THE THOUGHT TRAP

Walled gardens and online propaganda are eating our minds

Nate Levesque

Additional Information

The views expressed in this book are solely those of the author. They are not influenced by and do not reflect the views of any affiliations of the author other than by pure coincidence.

If at any point you find a factual error or poorly chosen source, you can make your concerns heard at www.natelevesque.com/factcheck.

This is an independently published work and your support is appreciated.

THE THOUGHT TRAP

CONTENTS

THE FRONT LINES

1 · THE COLLABORATORS

> All the army forces inside and outside the
> barracks, assemble. Read our command
> carefully before the raid.
>
> [...]
>
> Don't comment. Don't curse. Just report them.[1]

Khmer Krom News was attacked on July 12th, 2014. But,
no formal military was involved and not a single
gunshot would be fired. Pro-government forces wanted
to disrupt the independent Vietnamese news site and
cut it off from its audience. The weapon of choice for
the raid was Facebook's "Report Abuse" button,
commandeered by vigilantes to get *Khmer Krom News'*
Facebook page taken offline for being overly critical of
the government.

Facebook has become a battleground for civilian
thought police all over the world. Groups like the one
that attacked *Khmer Krom News* have found they can

abuse the moderation tools social media provide to us to censor and disrupt content they disagree with—right in the open. They build armies of fake accounts and coordinate virtual raids on content they disagree with to report it as offensive as many times as possible. It's hard for social media to catch these fake accounts before they make reports, and it doesn't matter if they're caught after because they only need to survive for a short time to do damage. Individuals involved in social media raids brag about the numbers of fake accounts they created for raids. One member of the *Khmer Krom News* raid said "I set up dozens of accounts for this =))"[2] in a Facebook comment thread for planning the attack, apparently not worried that Facebook might notice.

As of the end of 2014, Vietnamese groups reported that the accounts of 44 journalists and activists, as well as those of various publications had been pushed offline. Some, such as journalist Pham Doan Trang, suggested the numbers were actually much higher, in the hundreds.[3] Of course, Vietnamese groups are not the only targets. Syrian and Russian activists have faced take-downs for years that they have attributed to similar raids.[4] For most pages, the take-down is a major, but temporary disruption. For some, it's permanent.

Facebook says that only content that violates its guidelines is permanently removed, and that getting content taken down is not as easy as it seems. The report button is only one factor of many in its decisions about content removals. According to Facebook, "convincing lots of people to report something won't cause the information to be taken down or hidden unless there's something else about it that violates our policies."[5] However, that hasn't stopped groups from trying and, seemingly, from succeeding.

But, we can't blame only vigilante idea defenders for causing problems. When moderation works as intended, it keeps our news feeds and comments clear of overly offensive or graphic content. Any post a site doesn't catch—or just anything we find distasteful—can be reported with a handy "Report Abuse" button somewhere on or near it. After enough reports, a site might remove the content and ban the offending page or user. Some services allow the subject of the ban to appeal the decision, others use a three-strikes style system, while still others have little to no mercy. On some sites, the author of the post might never be told that it was taken down.

Although as individuals most of us don't participate in organized Facebook raids, we, too, are involved with harmful content take-downs. The Report Abuse button can be just as harmful as social media raids when used in the way social sites intend. Those of us in stable regions don't often consider the role Facebook plays in our lives and how it its role might differ for those in other parts of the world. So, from our safe homes we report graphic content like our social networks tell us we should. We're unknowingly causing problems.

The downside of those reports and subsequent take-downs is that graphic content we find offensive might be valuable to others. Social media has become a way for human rights activists in war-torn regions to publicize evidence of human rights abuses and other atrocities—and we're fighting those efforts. Social media allows content to be shared to the world easily from places where there is a high likelihood that the data—or the person who created it—won't survive. For people in those areas, social media is a tool to preserve information and get it out of the country to people who are able to take action on it, not just a place for sharing cat pictures.

Human rights workers and courts rely on that social media evidence to document atrocities and to bring cases against their perpetrators. In 2016, Facebook videos of an ISIS fighter posing with decapitated prisoners helped lead to a guilty verdict in Germany.[6] During the summer in 2017, the International Criminal Court (ICC) put out an arrest warrant for a Libyan commander for extrajudicial killings, based partly on videos posted to Facebook.[7] Take-downs, however well-meaning, are causing problems for these cases and for human rights groups. Much of this data is irreplaceable, and sometimes we're part of the reason it disappears.

In January 2014 a man named Abdulsalam found his morning prayer in al-Bab, Aleppo interrupted by a Syrian bomb. Abdulsalam, who worked with a group of activists to document and publicize the Syrian civil war, was among the first on the scene. Before joining the rescue effort, he took photos to document the destruction. Later that day he uploaded the pictures to Facebook in hopes of preserving them, unsure when his computer or camera might be destroyed in an attack. At the time the photos were taken, investigators from Human Rights Watch (HRW) were no longer able to collect their own evidence on the ground in the area,[8] so Abdulsalam's photos might have been valuable to them.

Facebook users around the world reported the photos for their graphic content as the social site encourages its users to do. Months later, Abdulsalam received an email from Facebook. Facebook, due to the reports of graphic content, had taken the photos down. When it did, the last copies were lost because the camera and hard drive with Abdulsalam's copies had been destroyed when the Islamic State raided al-Bab. It's possible the photos could have been used to help address the atrocities they documented. Abdulsalam's story is not uncommon.

Facebook, as with many social sites, walks many narrow lines with its content guidelines because it needs to adhere to the laws of each country it operates in, while supporting free speech. The site has been under fire for not being restrictive enough when groups such as ISIS use it to spread extremist propaganda, as well as for being too restrictive such as when it banned the ACLU's page over a post about censorship. Most social media services find themselves in a similar place.

What's allowed is ultimately up to the site it's posted on, based on the site's morals, its legal obligations, and its branding choices.

Like Facebook, YouTube has policies about graphic or extremist content and, similarly, has been under fire for being either too restrictive or not restrictive enough depending on the content. Between October and December 2017, YouTube's algorithms flagged 6.7 million uploaded videos for review by moderators. Of those, 76% were removed before a single user viewed them.[9] Censored videos included everything from "Tide Pod Challenges," to adult content, to graphic extremism. YouTube offered little transparency into how it decided what it would allow, and had no real oversight aside from community outrage which the site occasionally appeared to ignore.

The same year, YouTube and Facebook faced outcry for censoring videos that documented atrocities. Some 900 YouTube channels from groups and individuals were shut down nearly overnight, including ones run by reputable organizations like Bellingcat and AirWars, as well as media organizations run from Syria.[10] Facebook started removing images that documented the ethnic cleansing and torture of the Rohingya minority under the Myanmar government because, like with Abdulsalam's photos, users had flagged them as graphic content.[11] While the censored content was indeed graphic, it was the work of people and organizations trying to document human rights violations in the best ways they could.

This is a far cry from the goals of the Internet and of the sites themselves, which promised to be platforms of openness and accountability. In 2013, Facebook CEO Mark Zuckerberg declared connectivity to be a human right and Google's Schmidt wrote in *The New Digital Age*, "anyone with a mobile handset and access to the Internet will be able to play a part in promoting accountability."

Unfortunately, it appears the realities of promoting accountability don't fit with the content guidelines social media now has in place. Inadvertently, everyday social media users like ourselves may be helping to censor human rights violations by doing exactly what social media sites suggest when we come across graphic content—report it as abusive. We don't fully understand the repercussions of doing so, because social sites haven't really told us what happens to content they take down.

Facebook and YouTube have both defended their handling of potential evidence of war crimes posted to their platforms, and have promised to do better. In a 2016 blog post, Facebook said it was "looking forward to working closely with experts, publishers, journalists, photographers, law enforcement officials and safety advocates"[12] to find out how it could do better about what content it took down. YouTube made a similar statement that explained the site "[was] committed to ensuring human rights activists and citizen journalists have a voice on YouTube."[13]

Despite the sites' promises, human rights activists were still deeply concerned about content take-downs. A senior trial lawyer at the International Criminal Court responsible for prosecuting war criminal cases told *The Intercept* "it's something that keeps me awake at night, the idea that there's a video or photo out there that I could use, but before we identify it or preserve it, it disappears."[14] Seventy-three rights organizations have called on Facebook to clarify its removal policies around content, "especially human rights documentation."[15]

The battle of the take-downs is a realization of how powerful social media is for controlling content and for affecting opinion—and bigger players are noticing. Although many Facebook raids are from volunteer citizens, governments are also starting to realize the power of social media in managing opinion. Some, including *Khmer Krom News'* home, Vietnam, employ digital commentators who provide a pro-government presence in social media conversations. Vietnam ran a propaganda office with some 1,000 "public opinion shapers" as of 2013[16] and deployed 10,000 "cyber warriors" in 2017 to fight "wrongful views."[17] Their job was to spread party propaganda to manipulate public opinion and quell dissent—including pushing misinformation that opposed human rights and democracy activists, supported by volunteers.

Vietnam is not alone in involving itself in social media.

Around the world, governments have asked social media to moderate content on their services for various reasons. In December 2015, Twitter, Facebook, and Google reached an agreement with the German government that required the companies to take down illegal hate speech within 24 hours of its posting. Though Facebook has neither confirmed nor denied the statement, a senior Israeli cabinet minister announced the Israeli government and Facebook "agreed to work together to determine how to tackle incitement on the social network" and later the same month Facebook disabled the accounts of several people involved with two Palestinian publications.[18]

When governments make agreements with our social sites, however well-meaning they may be for tackling hate speech or harassment, they bypass the transparency we expect in public policy. They leave both judgment and enforcement up to the inner workings of the companies behind the social platforms. Few sites give us much insight into how or why their moderation systems make decisions, and sometimes don't tell us if they've made a decision at all.

It's hard for us to be heard in these issues. In theory, we can take our data to other places when we disagree with how our social media services handle content or privacy. We have the option to use whatever social platform suits our ethics, but there are clear dominant players in the social media space. Moving to a different social media site than our friends are not starts to defeat the purpose of being on social media.

But, we can only make ourselves heard and try to convince the sites we use to do better when we know what's going on. Lack of transparency and leaving both judging and enforcing content violations up to sites makes it difficult for anyone not employed by a network to know if a network is acting in good faith. We know important content has vanished from social networks with no due process—sometimes in political social media raids we may not fully understand—and we don't know what policies social sites will choose to adopt in the future. Laws, agreements, and corporate leadership can change the priorities of a company. Content can be and has been taken down retroactively, so just because a site allows something to stay for now, there is no guarantee it will be there in the future. The platforms we trust—even when they tell us our memories are important to them—can rewrite history within the bounds of their services, and we may not notice. If that history isn't to our liking, we may be able to find a lot of friends to report it and it might just disappear.

2 · THE MODERATORS

Earlier today, Cloudflare terminated the account of the Daily Stormer. We've stopped proxying their traffic and stopped answering DNS requests for their sites. We've taken measures to ensure that they cannot sign up for Cloudflare's services ever again.

[...]

In a not-so-distant future, if we're not there already, it may be that if you're going to put content on the Internet you'll need to use a company with a giant network like Cloudflare, Google, Microsoft, Facebook, Amazon, or Alibaba—Matthew Prince, Cloudflare CEO[1]

In the wake of the August 2017 Charlottesville riots in the U.S. during which a neo-Nazi rally met with protesters and turned violent leading to riots, dozens of injuries, and three deaths, everyone rushed to distance themselves from anything related to the neo-Nazi cause. Companies ranging from the tiki-torch manufacturers whose torches were used in the rally, to web hosting companies that found themselves in the awkward position of hosting neo-Nazi websites, published statements.

Hosting providers found themselves in a particularly difficult position because they were part of the reason the groups had a voice. As part of longstanding traditions of neutrality, as long as content was legal, the providers allowed it on their networks. Although they had the power and the right to take down neo-Nazi content they didn't want to host, they opted to leave it online no matter how much they disagreed with its message. But, they were aware of the PR nightmare that could cause them after Charlottesville and were watching carefully. GoDaddy, a domain name registration company used by the neo-Nazi site *Daily Stormer*, took issue with an article the site posted after the riots.

The content from the *Stormer* that pushed GoDaddy over the line was a vulgar post attacking Heather Heyer, one of the fatalities of the riots. GoDaddy told the *Daily Stormer* it had 24 hours to move its domain name registration elsewhere, as the company would no longer provide services for it. The hosting provider explained that it was dropping the site because it had endorsed violence, which was a violation of the GoDaddy terms of service. Some groups questioned

GoDaddy's reasoning for dropping the site, as the *Stormer* had a history of calling for genocide that the hosting service ignored. GoDaddy reaffirmed its stance on free speech in its statement about pushing the *Stormer* off its service.

> While we detest the sentiment of this site and the article in question, we support First Amendment rights and, similar to the principles of free speech, that sometimes means allowing such tasteless, ignorant content.
>
> In instances where a site goes beyond the mere exercise of these freedoms, however, and crosses over to promoting, encouraging, or otherwise engaging in violence against any person, we will take action. In our determination, especially given the tragic events in Charlottesville, Dailystormer.com crossed the line and encouraged and promoted violence.[2]

Google followed suit when the neo-Nazi site tried to move its registration from GoDaddy's services, and the *Daily Stormer* subsequently lost its .com domain name.[3] The site reappeared briefly after registering a Russian domain name with a Russian registrar. But, that wasn't the end of its trouble. Zoho, its email provider, cut ties too. So did Cloudflare, which provided security services to the *Stormer*, by cancelling the site's account and ignoring requests for its website. The neo-Nazi site was nearly forced offline, no longer able to find a company willing to power its content.[4]

Like GoDaddy, Cloudflare had a longstanding tradition of neutrality. Its move to drop the *Daily Stormer* signalled a change in the company's position of free-speech absolutism which it had just reaffirmed 3 months before the riots. The company's announcement for its actions from CEO Matthew Prince included some reflection that after the chain of events, rang true. A handful of companies had almost pushed a controversial website off the Internet, with little warning. They could do the same to any website.

> Without a clear framework as a guide for
> content regulation, a small number of
> companies will largely determine what can and
> cannot be online.[5]

To be very clear, this is not a defense of the *Daily Stormer*. The site is listed as a hate group by the Southern Poverty Law Center and borrows its name from a Nazi propaganda newspaper titled Der Stürmer. It's one of the most openly racist websites on the web, spreads racist, homophobic, and antisemitic propaganda, conspiracy theories, and celebrates the Holocaust while carefully staying on the side of legality. Its target audience is not only adults who have been tangled in neo-Nazi ideas, but minors who lack the perspective to know better. *Daily Stormer* editor Andrew Anglin has explained the purpose of the site is to attract young audiences. "My site is mainly designed to target children. Eleven through teenage years.... Young adults, pubescents."[6]

Much of the Internet was happy to see a site like the *Daily Stormer* find its near demise at the hands of hosting providers. Activist groups celebrated the dropping of the site as an unquestionable victory in keeping blatant racism out of civil online discourse. Cloudflare, GoDaddy, Google, and other companies involved in the take-downs were the Internet's heroes of the day. However, the actions of those companies raised questions about the roles of hosting providers and other services in an ecosystem that promises but doesn't guarantee free speech in the way many of us expect.

Digital rights and free speech advocates had varied reactions to the dropping of the *Stormer*. The Electronic Frontier Foundation's (EFF) Senior Information Security Counsel Nate Cardozo supported GoDaddy's right to drop customers it disagreed with but also explained "we feel that the infrastructure that serves up the internet must remain neutral."[7] The Oakland-based Center for Media Justice's director, Malkia Cyril, saw free speech as a distraction from the issue. "Cutting off sponsorship of violent white supremacy isn't corporate censorship. It's a positive assertion of values and a clear rebuke of domestic terrorism."[8]

Cyril had a point. Moderation, in any form it might come in, is an unfortunate obligation for much of the Internet's services. The web, especially its social side, provides cover and courage for people who intend to harass someone or disparage a group, as well as a platform for spreading hateful ideas. We see this in the comment sections of most websites, and various communities joke about what might be found in the comments (others recommend never visiting them). Moderation protects us from the worst humanity has to offer. But, it isn't an easy job—with regard to the content human moderators have to contend with, as well as the decisions about what types of things need to be taken down.

> Mora-Blanco won't describe what she saw that morning. For everyone's sake, she says, she won't conjure the staggeringly violent images which, she recalls, involved a toddler and a dimly lit hotel room.[9]

The content YouTube moderator Mora-Blanco blocked from appearing was illegal by every definition, but other content is not as easy to categorize. Hate speech, in particular, can be a problem. What's difficult about hate speech is where to draw the line as to what constitutes hateful content because what hate speech means evolves with time and gets decided by the majority, which risks policies becoming outdated and minority views being stifled. It's a balancing act for social sites. Reddit, for example, typically allows hateful conversations because the site is a strong proponent of free speech, though does have policies around certain things and periodically removes hate-based communities from its service.

Even so, keeping true hate speech under control matters

because it can incite violence, even if it doesn't explicitly call for it. Keegan Hankes, an analyst at the Southern Poverty Law Center's Intelligence Project pointed to the Charleston, South Carolina shooter who murdered nine African Americans during a prayer service in 2015 as an example. The shooter credited his "awakening" to materials posted by a white supremacist group. "He acted on what he saw as a concerted attack against the white race, and he thought that because he spent hours online reading this propaganda."[10] A 2018 shooting at Pittsburgh synagogue Tree of Life had similar motivations, based on a post from its perpetrator: "[Hebrew Immigrant Aid Society] likes to bring invaders in that kill our people. I can't sit by and watch my people get slaughtered. Screw your optics, I'm going in."[11]

Fringes of the online community will find a way to spread hate content even after the worst tragedies. In the aftermath of the 2015 Charleston, South Carolina, church shooting, posts appeared on racist Reddit communities that called the shooter "one of us"[12] and claimed the lives of people of color were worthless.[13]

As of the end of 2018, Facebook had about 15,000 people working to moderate content posted to its service. For employees of Cognizant, a company Facebook contracts with for content moderation, it's a thankless job that pays only $28,800 a year and comes with panic attacks and PTSD. It also comes with a constant onslaught of hate, graphic porn, and conspiracy theories—to name a few things. *The Verge* painted a grisly picture of what it was like to be a moderator in a 2019 article, a rare look at an industry hidden behind contracts and non-disclosure agreements.[14]

The push by online services to curb hate speech and harassment is driven by just how frequently the issues are seen across the Internet. Roughly four in ten Americans have personally experienced harassment online, including 18% of Americans who have experienced physical threats, sustained harassment, stalking, or sexual harassment.[15] Hate speech, defined as online harassment focused on disabilities, sexual orientation, race, religion, or gender, is seen with similar frequency, especially on anything even remotely related to those themes.

The issue extends off the Internet and causes real problems for victims. In a 2016 survey, 38% of harassment victims reported it hurt their self-esteem, 29% said it caused them to fear for their lives, and 20% reported it made them afraid to leave their home.[16] Children who are victims of online harassment are three times more likely to consider committing suicide.[17] Tools to counter online harassment, such as the report abuse button, need to continue to improve to ensure we don't fall victim to people who intend to use the platforms maliciously. At the same time, social networks need to protect against the people who use those features maliciously.

Although services promise neutrality, we don't always know what their reason for taking down content is. Some are concerned with the type of communities their platforms attract. Some are concerned with the advertising revenue that keeps them afloat, if not profitable. Others simply want to keep their users safe and provide a consistent experience. Their moderation decisions vary depending on their motives and their platforms, and their actions range from advertising restrictions to outright bans. Sometimes, rules change with little warning to the community they effect, and many of us get caught in the aftermath.

When they choose to moderate content, services have an extraordinary amount of power over what's online. Social networks can make content permanently disappear with little to no warning. Domain registrars and hosting providers have the power to make entire websites disappear—or point their addresses somewhere else entirely—in minutes. We generally assume they will remain neutral, or that they will use that power to society's benefit. However, it's naive to assume companies will only act in the best interests of the Internet. With the case of the *Daily Stormer*, the companies that dropped the site violated their own promises in response to public pressure and PR concerns. Although it may have been a positive assertion of values, as Cyril said, it was a reminder of their power over our digital content.

In early 2017, YouTube tightened content guidelines to

prevent advertisers from having their names associated with controversial content. As part of the change, it demonetized (removed ads from) videos that were explicit, sexually suggestive, violent, or that dealt with certain controversial content. In late 2017, YouTube further tightened its guidelines for demonetization, and updated its moderation algorithms to match. Channels that included controversial content, explicit language, or off-color humor found themselves at risk of being stripped of ad revenue. Some saw their revenue drop by as much as 80%.[18] The YouTube community spoke out against the changes because some creators relied on YouTube as their primary income.

The new policies caused changes to the YouTube community, as well as the format of YouTube videos. The threat of demonetization was an indirect way of censoring video content and led to changes—not only to avoid demonetization, but to make up for it. Over 2018, YouTube creators started to look for other ways to make money on their videos. Some built ads into their videos with direct advertising deals, adding promotional mentions to their normal videos so demonetization mattered less. Others turned to subscription models via sites like Patreon, where their fans could directly pay them for content with recurring subscription fees—sometimes adding their donors to end credits to encourage people to sign up.

Blogging site Tumblr took a harder approach to changing its content guidelines when it updated them in late 2018—it outright banned and removed content that was in violation of new guidelines. The change was in response to Apple temporarily dropping the Tumblr app from the App Store due to accusations that Tumblr was not taking actions to prevent illegal pornography from being posted. On December 17th, 2018, Tumblr banned all adult content from its site with only a few weeks warning. CEO Jeff D'Onofrio explained the changes in a December post on the Tumblr staff blog.

> We've given serious thought to who we want to be to our community moving forward and have been hard at work laying the foundation for a better Tumblr. We've realized that in order to continue to fulfill our promise and place in culture, especially as it evolves, we must change. Some of that change began with fostering more constructive dialogue among our community members. Today, we're taking another step by no longer allowing adult content, including explicit sexual content and nudity (with some exceptions).[19]

Tumblr wasn't a service that specifically catered to adult content, but also didn't forbid it provided that it was properly tagged. As such, porn communities developed on Tumblr, especially for the LGBTQ+ community and various niche interests. The legal porn communities pushed the blogging site to treat its porn community responsibly and asked for action against porn bots and illegal content, but the site allegedly never acknowledged the requests.[20] Without the necessary focus on moderating that type of content, Tumblr developed a circle of illegal content that the site either ignored or failed to notice until Apple took action.

The policy change shook many of the communities on the site whose members weren't sure where to turn after relying on Tumblr for years. Although porn made up only an estimated 0.1% of the content on the site, data scientists estimated that a quarter of Tumblr's users were there to consume it.[21] Though some concern was overblown and Tumblr as a service would survive, the community as it existed before the ban would not. As a side effect, communities that planned to move away from Tumblr had the potential to influence other sites—PornHub, for one, pitched itself to the Tumblr community as an alternative home that supported both adult and non-adult blog content.[22]

There are concerns that certain moderation practices, especially legislatively driven ones, come with the potential to violate free speech. Most online services, social media included, promise to be neutral venues for speech but have varying policies around how free speech on their platforms really is. However, decrying (or ignoring) any potential censorship claims, the online community at large continues to push social sites to better counter hate. And, with the Charlottesville riots, public pressure opened a new way for anything perceived as hate speech to be censored when web infrastructure companies added themselves to the content moderation movement.

All of this is legal. Companies are within their rights to choose what is and is not allowed on their platforms. The actions of those companies, even to take an entire site offline, are not violations of the First Amendment according to current U.S. laws. Wayne Giampietro, a Chicago First Amendment lawyer explained, "hate speech can't be a crime because it is protected by the First Amendment. But the First Amendment doesn't apply to people who run the internet."[23] Service providers have rights to free speech just like we do— and therefore editorial control—if they're not classified as common carriers.

It may be legal, but it may affect us in negative ways. Not everyone can pack their bags and move their content to PornHub when their posts suddenly violate their social network's guidelines. Overly strict content guidelines and terms of service agreements can limit our speech and impact the communities that use a service. We need moderation because not everyone on the Internet is a good person. But, we also need to know when we're subject to moderation and what the details of it are. Whether it's the actions of a faceless social media algorithm or an infrastructure provider, it's hard to know how the bounds of free speech on the Internet, or when some speech will suddenly no longer be welcome on a platform. And, even though PornHub pitches itself as a place for free speech, even its service has guidelines and content bans which are needed to keep its own community legal and reasonably safe.[24]

3 · THE DIVIDERS

The filter bubble tends to dramatically amplify confirmation bias—in a way, it's designed to. Consuming information that conforms to our ideas of the world is easy and pleasurable; consuming information that challenges us to think in new ways or question our assumptions is frustrating and difficult. This is why partisans of one political stripe tend not to consume the media of another. As a result, an information environment built on click signals will favor content that supports our existing notions about the world over content that challenges them—Eli Pariser[1]

"The 'Filter Bubble' Explains Why Trump Won and You Didn't See It Coming" *New York Magazine* said after the 2016 election. *Wired* told us our filter bubbles were "destroying democracy."[2] "Forget Facebook and Google, burst your own filter bubble" *Digital Trends* suggested. All those headlines were certain of one thing —that we're ideologically isolated from each other due to the content curation of the services we get our information from. And, they could be right. We are exposed to different realities, in customized feeds on some sites that adapt themselves based on what we look at.

Our filter bubbles as they're called—a term coined by Eli Pariser in his 2011 book—are a combination of automated processes and our online activities. The algorithms that build our feeds learn about us based on the things we click on the most, who we talk to, and what and who we choose to follow. They then suggest more content that's similar. Each of our feeds is specific to us and our beliefs. Our resulting digital realities keep us from seeing a whole picture of our world.

Often, algorithms decide what to show us based on the things we click, but as they show us fewer things outside our bubble, we'll click those things less—which makes the walls of our bubbles thicker. Did Donald Trump win the popular vote in the 2016 election, or did Hillary Clinton? Does a search for "BP" turn up the Deepwater Horizon oil spill or investment news about BP? For those of us stuck in a bubble, the answer to those questions might be different.

As our bubbles closed around us, we either welcomed it —because it gave us better recommendations from our digital assistants—or we didn't notice it—because it made our feeds more comfortable. Confronting our beliefs, and why they differ from those of others, is hard. Our social feeds reaffirm our values, whatever they might be. It's relatively rare for our feeds to show opposing views because our behavior is a disincentive for sites to show them to us.

The walls of our bubbles may thicken or weaken depending on our real world group of friends, where we live (or where we came from), and our level of privilege in both our physical and digital worlds. Online it's easy to thicken the walls of our bubble. With the addition of "unfollow" and "mute" features in the places where we might find viewpoints other than our own, hiding those views from ourselves without unfriending someone is easier than ever. It's a common practice. Whether it's alright to unfollow someone we disagree with even made it into an opinion-piece question published by *The Guardian* (the answer was no, but not because the author felt it would expand our world view). Sometimes, we might go even further and move to a different social community altogether to find content that matches our interests and values. As early as 2009, Pew Research observed we were moving away from sites with no political affiliation to those that aligned with our own views.[3]

A study published in 2017 illustrated that effect on Twitter. Tweets that were morally outraged were re-tweeted mostly within circles that agreed with them, and saw little traction elsewhere.[4] Even the most moral, emotional, and well-crafted tweet, it seemed, rarely had the power to be retweeted across the political aisle. The story was similar on other platforms—Facebook showed different content to different sides of the political spectrum, and Tumblr and Reddit provided targeted advertisements that did the same thing.

The fact that many of our online worlds are heavily targeted is no secret. Facebook talks about interest targeting in its help center and Google offers settings for news and ad targeting—it's a feature that's sold to us. Some sites even let us turn it off—though they recommend we leave it on for, in their words, a better experience. When we're subject to it, we don't know is what's hidden or why because most sites keep their algorithms secret.

That's not to say our targeted reality is completely wrong—we do get breaking news and other relevant information. Localizing our content can give us more relevant news—what's going on in our own city might at times be more important or relevant than the latest headlines from the other side of the world. However, it's incomplete. The content we see might be missing important news because our feeds decided we wouldn't be interested in it. We might only see content with a particular spin. Or, worse, our feeds might be more susceptible to fake news, targeted in such a way that those who would know it as such would never see it, so we would never be warned that it was fake.

The negative side effects of targeting generally aren't the intent. Ad revenue drives the bottom line of most free-to-use services, and more effective personalization gives sites better numbers. That is, they're usually not trying to push us towards a particular view. Instead, they're just giving us reflections of ourselves which over time makes differing opinions seem more extreme. We might be tricked into feeling more connected with our world thanks to confirmation bias, but the opposite is true. Pariser explained that interest targeting was, itself, apolitical.

> They don't overtly take a stance, they invisibly
> paint the digital landscape with things that are
> likely to align with your point of view.[5]

The divisive nature of our filter bubbles is most obvious when it comes to news and politics, especially with the 2016 U.S. election. A post titled "Why I'm Voting for Donald Trump" was shared over 1.5 million times on Facebook. Another, titled "There are five living U.S. presidents. None of them support Donald Trump." was shared 1.7 million times.[6] Depending on which way Facebook thought someone leaned politically, they likely only saw one or the other and only saw content related to the one they saw. This is part of the reason why the fact that Hillary Clinton won the popular vote so substantially and the fact that Donald Trump became president were so shocking to their respective opposing sides.

It's a widespread issue and it's growing as we rely increasingly on social sites to give us headlines—and it really does affect all of us. 62% of U.S. adults got at least some of their news on social media in 2016,[7] and were subjected to targeted content. The effect doesn't care who we are. Everyone, from us, to our thought leaders, to our journalists, to yes, myself, has a filter bubble. What makes it through our bubbles influences what we think, share, and write about—even on the scale of covering the news or publishing a book. It makes it harder for us to connect with and to understand people who might think differently from us. Pariser hit on that too.

> A wider problem is that with such difference sources of information between people, it can lead to the generation of a real disconnect, as they become unable to understand how anyone could think differently from themselves.[8]

Some research suggests our filter bubbles may not be as polarizing as we have been led to believe, but visualizations of how ideas spread on Twitter and the fact that two sides of the political spectrum appear to have seen very different content in 2016 indicate there is some effect, though perhaps not a well understood one. Pariser himself said he has "always been worried about over-claiming what social media is doing to us now."[9]

However, Pariser also believed the effect was growing, and we can see why. The web that helped former president Barack Obama reach supporters in 2008 was a much less personalized and much less divisive place. With a thinner bubble and more suspicion around social networks, people were more inclined to fact check what they saw.

Today, the web is very different. The social media landscape is far from finished evolving, and we don't know how it could look years from now. As Pariser put it, "We haven't yet reached the event horizon where social media is the primary driver of how we consume things. I still believe that across that event horizon are strange and scary phenomena."[10] Microsoft co-founder Bill Gates told *Quartz* of concerns as well. "One thing that's new that is a little concerning is people seeking out things that are really not giving them the facts, and then staying in there."[11]

What that event horizon will look like depends on how much respect the sites that build our feeds have for neutrality and news—and democracy. If social media succeeds in adding news to the social media diet of morally outraged posts and cat pictures, the future of social media could be less bleak than what Pariser and many others envision. But with ad-revenue incentives a heavy influence, there's no guarantee information will get the respect it needs. We don't know how news will spread through our filter bubbles as social media takes a bigger role in its distribution. So far, experiments that added news to our feeds have had mixed results, from unexpected changes to news feed algorithms to accusations of bias. Nonetheless, tech companies have pressed on. But, even social media doesn't know how things will or should look, and they have sometimes made unpredictable moves to add and remove news features.

Facebook announced a program in 2011 for news outlets to create "social reader" applications which highlighted their content in the Facebook feed. *The Washington Post* found success from the program, which drew millions more readers to its articles. In April 2012, more than four million people were using its social reader app—but the program wasn't as successful for Facebook as the social giant hoped. So, Facebook updated its algorithms again, this time to show less news, and within just three days *The Washington Post* saw the number of users of its social reader app drop from four million to almost zero. Eventually, Facebook did away with the social reader apps altogether.[12]

In 2013, Facebook tried again. The company made changes to its news feed to show more news and current events, giving it a foothold for being a force in online journalism—filter bubbles and all.[13] But, it didn't stop there.

A year later, Facebook launched its infamous "trending topics" feature to highlight popular news. Speculation from *TechCrunch* when it was announced suggested that it could get Facebook "known as a news source for news and current events."[14] Two years after its release, Facebook found the feature at the center of a controversy about its neutrality. According to some former employees, conservative news and news about Facebook itself were routinely prevented from appearing in the trending headlines.[15] Others described orders to artificially add headlines even if they hadn't seen enough traction to be automatically included. In some cases, headlines that were added artificially became the trending news on Facebook.[16]

In 2015, amidst the controversy over the trending topics feature, the social network started to encourage news outlets to host content on Facebook itself with "Instant Articles" that promised to improve user experience and therefore views.[17] Although bringing quality, reliable news to social feeds is a noble goal, the approach also gave Facebook more control over consumption of news, and control over how we interacted with it.

To counter those issues, Facebook fired the human teams responsible for curating the content and replaced them with algorithms that picked the true top news trending on the site. Unfortunately, Facebook assumed the topics trending on its service would be accurate. The software made little distinction between misinformation and real news, so fake news occasionally appeared in the trending topics. After a final attempt to fix the feature by requiring a topic to be covered by multiple news sources, Facebook removed the feature in 2018.[18]

However, Facebook was not the only giant working on news—nor was it finished.

In 2017, Google updated its mobile search app with a new set of features, which included a feed that resembled Facebook's. Google touted the updates as faster and easier ways for us to keep up with the things we cared about. However, it didn't make clear whether the feed was targeted. Google avoided answering questions about whether the app would show information that its users might disagree with.[19]

Aware of the criticism they had opened themselves to, Google and Facebook announced separate initiatives in 2017 and 2018 to improve their handling of news. Google introduced the Google News Initiative, which explained "Google cares deeply about journalism,"[20] and Facebook launched the Facebook Journalism Project.[21] Both initiatives appeared to indicate the companies were taking more responsibility for the news that appeared on their services through partnerships with news organizations. Neither appeared to address their platform's interest targeting when it came to news, though did include efforts for fighting fake news. The companies both said their initiatives would evolve to meet the needs of publishers and consumers of news.

Even if the initiatives don't address targeting and filter bubbles, we may not be at the point where we need them to. Our feeds do generally show us things we disagree with, despite the fact that they skew towards our own beliefs. In one study, roughly a third of the stories people interacted with in their Facebook feeds were opposed to their beliefs.[22] However, publishers have realized they can manipulate targeting in their favor by framing stories to fit with one narrative or another. The effect compounds. If we interact less with posts we don't agree with, we eventually stop seeing them so it takes an active effort to avoid falling into a filter bubble. We can only escape if we notice we're stuck—but that's getting harder while our digital world and our targeted feeds get more tightly integrated into our lives.

THE BUILDERS

4 · THE INTEGRATORS

Discontinued products and services are nothing new, of course, but what is new with the coming of the cloud is the discontinuation of services to which people have entrusted a lot of personal or otherwise important data – and in many cases devoted a lot of time to creating and organizing that data. As businesses ratchet up their use of cloud services, they're going to struggle with similar problems, sometimes on a much greater scale. I don't see any way around this – it's the price we pay for the convenience of centralized apps and databases – but it's worth keeping in mind that in the cloud we're all guinea pigs, and that means we're all dispensable. Caveat cloudster
—Nicholas Carr[1]

In 2013, as another piece of evidence to support Carr's description of the cloud, digital subscription service

Google Reader closed its doors. Fans of the service were upset by the decision. Carr too, an acclaimed technology, economics, and culture author, lamented Google Reader's fate on his personal blog shortly after the announcement.[2] For those who relied on the service, it was a big loss. The shutdown disconnected them from the people and websites they wanted to get updates from.

The closing of Google Reader was unsurprising in hindsight. RSS, the open data standard that Reader relied on, was designed for an earlier, more open Internet. Google saw the web evolving from its open and collaborative roots to a place where data was restricted to the platform it lived on. However, the evolution didn't start with Google Reader's demise and didn't end with it.

At the peak of open standards, there was an expectation that if a site allowed us to upload our data, it also allowed us to take it with us. Websites provided easy ways, such as RSS, ATOM, oEmbed, and other standards to share data and embed it in other sites. There was an acceptance of the idea that people might have an identity outside of a service, instead of relying on the profile pages inside. This came with a side effect which was good for the Internet in general but bad for the services with the data: it was possible to access content from a site without actually visiting that site and therefore, without seeing any of the ads that paid to keep that site online.

On the modern Internet, the experience is different. Many of the online giants provide relatively restricted (but wide-reaching) ecosystems. Facebook, Twitter, Reddit, and other social services are huge, but interact with each other only minimally. They want us to use the data in their ecosystems, but in ways that are profitable and in line with their branding. Getting things into the ecosystem works the same way. Each social network has a dedicated "share this" button that shows up across the Internet. We now have so many "share this" buttons that there are services such as AddThis and ShareThis dedicated to providing the full portfolio of social media buttons to web developers.

Although we can "share" to social media, taking content back out in any meaningful and portable way is getting harder. RSS and open data feeds still exist, but aren't widely used by the average person anymore. Mobile apps wrap the services we use—some of which don't exist outside an app—into separate boxes on devices that talk to each other only in specific ways, if at all. By restricting access, sites create a compelling reason for us to visit them by making themselves the only place data is available. Information in these ecosystems is less accessible to the rest of the Internet, which makes it harder to access and harder to find. Open web advocate Chris Saad described a sad picture of the Internet's evolution: "URLs are fading into the background, native mobile apps are all the rage and Facebook threatens to engulf the web into a proprietary black hole."[3]

We deal with this every day. Our smartphones give us access to the services on the mobile Internet, but we often have a separate app for each one we use. The services themselves are also isolated from each other. If we use Facebook while a friend uses Twitter, that's a no-go unless we both also use the opposing platform or look at things without interacting. It's worse when it comes to interest groups that operate primarily on a particular social network. Without using that platform, it's impossible to participate with the group—even if they're part of our real-world community.

As social networks have developed into fairly closed ecosystems, people who choose not to be a part of them have been cut off from communities they care about. Some groups rely on social media so much that their social media presence is the only place they exist online. Membership rosters, events, and even organization documents might be inside a closed ecosystem, which makes them unintentionally exclusionary. There is a distinct difference between being "connected" and being "open."

But, while technologies such as Saad and Carr lament a more open Internet, the evolution hasn't been entirely bad. Most of the proprietary services we use are generally pleasant places to spend time online—and they're usually safer than the Internet at large. As *Wired* founder and tech entrepreneur John Battale described it to *Fast Company*, "The open web is full of spam, shady operators and blatant falsehoods...In the curated gardens of places like Apple and Facebook, the weeds are kept to a minimum, and the user experience is just...better."[4] It's those walled gardens that allowed the Internet to expand to a place for everyone.

The walled gardens can and do offer open data, they just do so in a much more curated way—but that too is changing. At one point, social networks boasted about their open APIs (short for "application programming interfaces"), which provided ways for software and other websites to access their data. Facebook CEO Mark Zuckerberg announced in 2007, "right now, social networks are closed platforms, and today we're going to end that."[5] Twitter co-founder Biz Stone gave a similar announcement to *Readwrite* in 2008: "The API has been arguably the most important, or maybe even inarguably, the most important thing we've done with Twitter."[6]

Stone was right, APIs were a big deal. They let content out of the walled gardens and there were few limits to what creative things could be done with the data. Twitter's open API allowed people to mash up tweets relevant to a particular topic and analyze them, powering thousands of services such as *Politweets*, which aggregated tweets about the 2008 U.S. election.[7] Facebook's API powered 70 third-party applications when it launched in 2007, including ones from Amazon, Microsoft, Red Bull, and *The Washington Post*.[8] In 2013, web developer and author Jeremy Keith reflected on the open Internet on his website: "This was the era of the mashup—taking data from different sources and scrunching them together to make something new and interesting. It was a good time to be a geek."[9]

A year and a half after its announcement, Facebook changed its mind about its promise of openness and started restricting data, cutting off developers, and limiting its API.[10] In 2012, Twitter shared a similar new vision of its service that did not allow things on Twitter to be as easily taken elsewhere. Twitter's then-consumer product manager Michael Sippey touted new features, but also warned "[w]e've already begun to more thoroughly enforce our Developer Rules of the Road with partners, for example with branding, and in the coming weeks, we will be introducing stricter guidelines around how the Twitter API is used."[11] The same year, Twitter stopped letting Instagram users import their photos, and Instagram retaliated by stopping its users from importing their Twitter followers.[12]

Tech companies are well aware of the value of keeping people in their ecosystems and controlling content, which means the problem is likely to get worse. They're within their rights to lock down their platforms—and there can be good reasons to, because it's rarely a good thing to let the Internet at large have unrestricted access to services. And, they're taking it further than just restricting APIs. Facebook, Google, and other services have been working to integrate content creators, such as media outlets, directly into their platforms.

In 2015, Facebook announced "Instant Articles" which were intended to make the mobile web better. By loading content directly from Facebook's cloud, the experience on mobile is faster and uses less data.[13] The caveat, which Facebook sells to publishers as features, is that Facebook has a lot of control over Instant Articles. Facebook has control over much of the experience, can gather more information about what we're doing (some of which it shares with publishers), and starts integrating more content into Facebook. Facebook said it wouldn't give Instant Articles special treatment in its news feed. However, if Instant Articles worked well, they would likely see more traction from Facebook's users which might push publishers to use them more.

In response to Instant Articles, Google has been promoting a set of standards called AMP, originally short for Accelerated Mobile Pages, which are also intended to make content easier to consume on mobile.[14] The set of standards themselves, which Google collaborated with Twitter and other companies to create, are open source. In its stated goal, AMP works fairly well, serving stripped-down, simplified pages that load using less data and that work better on a mobile device. But, in a similar setup as Instant Articles, AMP allows Google to cache content so content loads from Google's cloud, meaning that while an article might be from a trusted news outlet, its visitors never leave Google. Google prioritizes AMP content in its search results. By hosting it, Google is integrating more content into its own walls where it can track exactly how people see it and control how they interact with it.

While they do improve our online experience, offerings like AMP or Instant Articles allow services to expand their reach into other areas of the Internet, and surreptitiously. The more integrated or closed a platform is, the more control the platform has over what people experience on it. Services want to build and control their entire relationship with their users, not just to provide a safer place online. It's also not good enough as-is. A 2019 proposal from Google intended to hide Google's involvement in serving AMP pages for users of Chrome by showing the original URL of an article instead of the AMP URL, with services like Cloudflare signing on to support the proposal.[15] While we don't know what the future holds for AMP or Instant Pages, we do know what other restricted ecosystems look like.

On a smaller scale, Google, Apple, and others already run curated ecosystems in which they can control everything. Apple, well-known for its curated ecosystem, can control most aspects of how its users experience its technology: what apps are available, how they look, and what they can do. The company even provides its own services for email, text messaging, cloud storage, and news, among other things. Similarly, Google provides everything from email to social networking to phone service, and exerts control over its own Google Play Store and Android devices. Once we've bought into one ecosystem, leaving for another takes a fair amount of work—and some things might get lost in the transition.

In restricting their ecosystems, tech companies began to change the nature of the Internet. Anil Dash, technologist, blogger, and entrepreneur, described "The Web We Lost" (also the title to his article) in 2012. He recalled Technorati's ability to search most of the social web from one place, the oEmbed format for embedding data from other sites, and days before monetized links. He was critical of the treatment services had shown the web.

> But they haven't shown *the web itself* the respect and care it deserves, as a medium which has enabled them to succeed. And they've now narrowed the possibilites [sic] of the web for an entire generation of users who don't realize how much more innovative and meaningful their experience could be.[16]

The walled gardens are growing, but not in the way we hoped. Their walls are getting taller as their APIs get more restricted, and they're enveloping more of the web through acquisitions. It's good for the companies that own the garden and occasionally for consumers, but less for the creators, startups, or small companies who have no choice but to be subjected to their restrictions and fees. The walled gardens are places where big parts of the Internet's users are, and that gives them a lot of control over how things work, and choosing to be excluded from them can be very limiting.

A company is within its rights to moderate its platform however it sees fit. If someone does something the service doesn't like (or that enough people report as offensive), that person and all their data can be kicked out of the garden. This is much more devastating than having a post taken down or missing a few posts that the service decided we wouldn't see. An ecosystem like Google's, which provides everything from social networking to email, can drop the majority of our digital life with a single ban. Getting banned by a large ecosystem like Google or Facebook can come at a high cost and with little to no warning.

Sometimes, it's about curating content, either who can see it or who can use it. Facebook, for example, provides free Internet service to underprivileged areas —however, it controls what websites are available on the service and as such, there are people who think Facebook is the Internet rather than a single service on it. Apple maintains strict control over what is allowed in the App Store. Twitter has turned off API access for apps it wasn't happy with, such as UberMedia in 2011 which Twitter said was infringing on trademarks and violating its terms of service.[17] And, Google has removed people from its ecosystem with little warning when it changed its mind about their content.

Dennis Cooper is an avant-garde writer and artist whose blog is a major online destination for fans of experimental literature. His work often depicts graphic violence and sexuality, themes that can be sensitive for some people. As such, his blog appropriately featured a warning and required visitors to consent to seeing adult content before they were able to access posts. In 2016, after fourteen years of hosting his blog, Google suspended Cooper's account and took down his blog without warning, apparently having decided his content no longer belonged in the company's ecosystem. Cooper also lost access to his Google-hosted email account and contact list, including offers to give talks and to perform.[18]

According to a Facebook post from Cooper, after months of negotiations between Cooper's lawyers and Google, Google agreed to return all the data that was taken down when they deactivated his account.[19] "As long as you back everything up. I don't see really the danger," Cooper told *The Guardian* at the time of the take-down. "But if you're at the mercy of Google or some place like Google, obviously I'm a living example of not to be blind like that and think that everything is hunky dory."[20]

Other times, tightening control and deepening integrations are about money. Apple charges a 30% fee to apps that sell things, which recently drove Netflix to stop allowing customers to sign up for its service through its iOS app. Amazon charges independent authors a 30% to 65% fee for selling books on its platform, depending on the book's list price and not counting paperback printing costs.[21] Although the fees

are high, simply not being there may not be an option—
Amazon is the dominant place to get e-books and
Apple is a significant share of the mobile device market
—and those fees, however high, pay for access as well
as the benefits the companies provide for publishing
through their services.

Changes to the gardens can drive apps—or entire
companies—out of business. 2011 was a bad year for e-
book apps for that reason, as companies including
Amazon and Apple changed their app arrangements.
The Lendle book-sharing service found its API access to
Amazon turned off without warning (though it was
restored after Lendle removed its ability to sync books
with Kindles).[22] The company behind iFlow Reader shut
down because it couldn't afford Apple's then-new 30%
fee on in-app sales.

> Apple is giving us the boot by making it
> financially impossible for us to survive. They
> want all of the eBook business on iOS and since
> they have the unilateral power to get it, we are
> out of business and the iFlow Reader is dead.
> We put our faith in Apple and they screwed
> us.[23]

But, that's not how the creators of the Internet wanted
things to be. As a community concerned about Google
AMP put it, "the Web is not Google, and should not be
just Google,"[24] a sentiment that could be extended to
almost any other household name in web giants. The
take-down of Cooper's Google account, the demise of

open data, and the shut-downs of companies due to app store changes show us how much the online world has changed. As the big players grow and extend their reach across the Internet, we find more of the web controlled by big entities who are free to limit speech and control standards however they want. It raises questions of content ownership, control, and responsibilities, and we haven't found answers to those questions yet. In the meantime, our rights to view and use data we rightfully have access to are eroding, including for data we might think we own.

5 · THE MERCHANTS

> The technology in question is an example of
> Digital Restrictions Management (DRM) --
> technology designed to restrict the public.
> Describing it as "copyright protection" puts a
> favorable spin on a mechanism intended to
> deny the public the exercise of those rights
> which copyright law has not yet denied them—
> Richard Stallman[1]

On a Friday in 2009, some Amazon customers discovered copies of George Orwell's *1984* and *Animal Farm* had mysteriously vanished from their Kindles as though illustrating a modern-day version of *1984*'s censorship themes. While this wasn't the only case of mysteriously vanishing books (copies of Harry Potter and Ayn Rand novels vanished at other times), it was interesting enough to hit the news because *1984* was involved.[2] It sparked discussions about censorship and ownership of digital goods, and the responsibilities of online services in respecting our access to data.

Amazon explained it had taken down certain copies of books that were published without authorization from copyright holders; *Animal Farm* is under copyright in the U.S. until 2041 and *1984* until 2044.[3] The company acknowledged that its move to delete the books from customer devices was a bad one and promised it would change its policies so remote deletions would no longer happen. But, in 2012 Amazon reignited the discussion by deleting the Amazon account of a Norwegian IT consultant and clearing all the books from her Kindle.[4] Though due to the much smaller incident of just one Kindle, Amazon was again subject to indignation from its e-reader customers who were concerned they could be next to lose their books.

The online retailer's actions were a reminder that companies which sell digital goods are within their rights to take back digital purchases. Their terms of service documents usually explain that when we buy digital content, we aren't buying the content in any way resembling buying a physical copy. Instead, the company is selling us access that can be revoked at any time. An excerpt from Amazon's terms of service in 2018 was quite explicit about who actually owned digital content from Amazon:

> All content included in or made available
> through any Amazon Service, such as text,
> graphics, logos, button icons, images, audio
> clips, digital downloads, data compilations, and

software is the property of Amazon or its
content suppliers and protected by United States
and international copyright laws. The
compilation of all content included in or made
available through any Amazon Service is the
exclusive property of Amazon and protected by
U.S. and international copyright laws.[5]

Amazon and other digital retailers are able to control
content that customers downloaded by controlling the
ecosystem that it was bought in, and by shipping it with
DRM. DRM, short for "digital rights management"
("digital restrictions management" to some, including
Richard Stallman who is a free software movement
activist and programmer), restricts how digital content
can be used. Its purpose is to limit what we can do with
whatever it was we bought digital access to in order to
protect the intellectual property rights of its creator.

The practice is relatively standard for digital content,
and it can come in a variety of forms. On a platform like
Steam or EA Origin, it handles digital distribution and
software licensing for games and other software. On
Amazon, Google Play, the Apple ecosystem, or the
Microsoft ecosystem, it might pertain to anything from
content to software. In the Amazon ecosystem, DRM on
e-books can stop us from taking books out of the
Amazon ecosystem, controls how or if we can lend
them, if a computer-generated narration is allowed, or
in some cases how many times they can be read. DRM
is often an optional feature driven by publishers, and is

normally not a required component for digital content. It can extend to anything involving software—John Deere uses it to prevent farmers from making "unauthorized" repairs to their own tractors.[6]

While the intent of DRM isn't necessarily bad, the ways it's put into practice often are. It sometimes forces us through cumbersome processes to access what we bought, and often restricts our freedoms in ways that are far more stringent than intellectual property laws. When it does, it makes content less accessible and less usable. By blocking text-to-speech software from reading an e-book, for example, that book becomes inaccessible to people with vision impairments—and may force people who need text-to-speech to pay extra for it. DRM also prevents some forms of Fair Use, such as backing up the e-book files on our devices in case something happens to them. Another form of DRM, region-locking, can make it hard to see content in our own language if we're abroad. The e-book format of this book is generally DRM free, depending on the bookstore you bought it from, in an effort to protect your freedoms.

Take-downs can happen on a large scale if DRM is involved, including for non-malicious reasons. Sometimes, the service powering the DRM might become obsolete. In April 2019, Microsoft announced it would shut down the DRM servers that were part of its e-book store and would issue refunds to its customers for anything they paid for on the service.[7] Refunds or not, as of July 2019 any books from Microsoft's service (including ones that were free) would no longer be accessible even if they were downloaded. Science fiction author and copyright activist Cory Doctorow discussed the shut down with *Motherboard* in an email:

> Microsoft once had an ebook store filled with 'buy now' buttons—today, Microsoft tells us that we never bought anything, that we merely conditionally licensed it.[8]

With total control over their ecosystems and with technologies like DRM, digital distributors have given themselves the ability to censor content for almost any reason. Most sites publish guidelines for what is and isn't allowed to be published on their platforms. But, their guidelines aren't always clear and like other moderation, their take-downs are sometimes inconsistent. There's little transparency in how content decisions are made or what happens to content that violates guidelines—even if we downloaded it. And, there are questions we need to consider, such as whether banned content should be taken away from us if it's already on our device, if the same should apply to malicious software or content.

The fact that companies can control things after we've bought them has allowed services to remove malicious apps from devices to protect users. Other times, like with Amazon's remote deletion of pirated copies of *1984* and *Animal Farm*, it allowed them to protect the intellectual property rights of creators by pulling back unauthorized copies of their work. Companies don't outright hide their ability to revoke access to or remotely delete content, though it's often buried in long terms of service documents that we tend to click through without reading.

As with most legitimate online stores, Amazon bans illegal, stolen, and copyright-infringing content. The retailer has reacted to public outcry on some take-downs, but there is no guarantee Amazon or another retailer would do that for something with more gravity if it felt the content was against its values.

Anything that doesn't fall under the umbrella of illegal, stolen, or copyright infringing material appears to be up to Amazon because the company's published policies have been inconsistent and sometimes overly broad. Amazon has selectively banned books for vague reasons, such as for certain pornographic content that wasn't specifically disallowed. In 2011, the online store's description of what was banned under the pornographic category was simply "pornography and hard-core material that depicts graphic sexual acts."[9]

Even Amazon seemed unsure of what its guidelines meant. Its broad definition seemingly stood counter to the fact that it had a category specifically for erotica books and films. The site developed a reputation for censoring erotica inconsistently and with little warning. In 2010, erotica author Esmeralda Greene published a blog post saying Amazon appeared to be taking down popular erotica titles written by herself and other independent authors, as well as some from major publishers.[10] *CBS News* observed similar inconsistencies due to the fact that sexually graphic independent films were for sale on Amazon despite the apparent general ban on pornographic content.[11]

In more recent versions of its content policies, Amazon improved its description of what constituted pornography. Other parts of the policy still have problems with specificity, which still leaves Amazon open to dropping other things as it sees fit. Amazon is well within its rights to do so, but as a site with a global reach and one that encourages creators to self-publish on its in-house service, it makes publishing some content on Amazon difficult.

Pornography

Pornography; X-rated movies; home porn; hard-core material, including magazines, that depict graphic sexual acts, amateur porn and soiled undergarments. Unrated erotic videos and DVDs and properly censored erotic artwork and magazines of the type you'd find at a typical bookstore are permitted. Nudity, graphic titles, and descriptions must be sufficiently concealed with censor strips on all items containing such content.

Offensive material

What we deem offensive is probably about what you would expect. This includes items such as crime-scene photos or human organs and body parts. Amazon.com reserves the right to determine the appropriateness of items sold on our site. Also, be aware of cultural differences and sensitivities. Some items may be acceptable in one country, but unacceptable in another. Please keep in mind our global community of customers.[12]

Other than a few mentions of specific types of content, Amazon's description of offensive material was not particularly helpful in determining what Amazon actually allows. There were few guidelines provided for what or how Amazon decided something was offensive, though made it clear it had complete discretion in deciding. That can be a problem because what might be considered offensive is often cultural—which Amazon's guidelines alluded to—and aren't the same from person to person. Guidelines that describe what's acceptable to publish on a platform need to be specific, especially when the platform is global. A mention of the Tiananmen Square massacre, for example, might make content unacceptable for China's policies, but not elsewhere.

When content violates guidelines, it can disappear in a variety of ways. Bans, take-downs, and remote deletions aren't the only tools to make content disappear. By dropping rankings and pushing things further down in search results—whether to the bottom of the page or all the way to the last page of results—

digital retailers can hide content or at least make it seem less appealing. In other cases, changing the product category can hide content elsewhere, such as by moving it to a less-visited or more restricted department.

In 2009, Amazon was caught doing this for certain LGBTQ+ related content, including leading LGBTQ+ books. Some books lost their sales rankings and others appeared to have been re-categorized as "Adult products."[13] The company blamed the problem on a glitch in its system, which was quickly fixed after the discovery. Whatever the intent or cause, the end result was that the books were less discoverable on Amazon until the problem was fixed, relegated to categories that implied non-adult LGBTQ+ content was sensitive for some audiences.

Amazon's policies and book removals matter because the retailer controls some 80% of the english e-book market according to an estimate from early 2017.[14] But, Amazon and e-books aren't the only concerns. Other types of content, such as mobile apps, can see similar problems with vague content policies. Digital distributors have cemented themselves as a primary way for us to consume the Internet and other digital content with mobile devices and the mobile app ecosystem.

Google and Apple control a combined 99.6% of the mobile device market[15] (though Google's Android is not always tied to the Google Play ecosystem). The two companies can control almost any aspect of the devices in their ecosystems, from remote-removal of content including apps, to locking out and wiping devices. While it is possible to load "unapproved" apps on a device, the process is somewhat cumbersome and devices have the option turned off by default. That means some banned content simply won't exist for the majority of people who use a mobile ecosystem that banned it.

In the wake of a late 2017 controversy around moderation policies in which a group of Twitter users accused Twitter of censoring conservative voices, a competing service called Gab emerged. Gab's premise was similar to Twitter but the service refused to censor any speech protected by the First Amendment, no matter how offensive. The new service quickly became popular for right-wing trolls and racists who were banned from Twitter after violating Twitter's rules.

Although the service gained traction among some users, its app wasn't well-received by app stores. Apple refused to publish the Gab app, cutting off the majority of iPhone and iPad users from easily using it. Google initially allowed the app to be installed from the Play Store, but later removed it citing violations of Google's hate speech policy and a lack of moderation.[16] Gab's founders defended their app by pointing out that other platforms, such as Twitter, also carried hate speech that could violate Google's terms of service.[17]

Services that are more popular and mainstream than Gab aren't safe from bans either. In late 2018, Apple temporarily dropped Tumblr's mobile app from the App Store after illegal pornographic content was discovered on a collection of Tumblr blogs. Popular messenger app Telegram was also temporarily removed from the App Store earlier the same year, for similar reasons, despite seeing 100,000 downloads per day.[18] While such take-downs might be the responsible thing to do under the circumstances, Telegram and Tumblr are both otherwise legitimate and reputable apps. Other times though, it's just business—Google and Microsoft had a disagreement over YouTube, so Google refused to authorize a YouTube app for the Microsoft Store.[19]

When our bookstores, our app stores, and our online ecosystems drop content, we need to know why. We rely on those ecosystems to keep us connected to our world. Digital platforms are the only places where a content ban can be almost perfectly enforced by not only removing content, but taking it away from us even, in some cases, if we downloaded it. They have the right to do it, and we gave them permission when we agreed to their terms of service. But, with vague content guidelines and little transparency around how our digital services decide what content gets kicked out, we're don't have all the information. Their decisions can influence us, and we're not empowered to know why.

6 · THE INFLUENCERS

> Mr. Stretch, you commented yesterday that your company's goal is bringing people together. In this case, people were brought together to foment conflict, and Facebook enabled that event to happen.
>
> I would say that Facebook has failed their goal. From a computer in St. Petersburg, Russia, these operators can create and promote events anywhere in the United States in attempt to tear apart our society—Senator Richard Burr[1]

In 2017, North Carolina Senator Richard Burr released a collection of 3,000 Facebook ads which revealed something disturbing. The ads painted a picture of how two Russia-based Facebook pages organized protests in Texas for opposing causes in the same place and at the same time, in an apparent attempt to start a conflict— and how they almost succeeded. On the day of the protests, the two groups escalated into confrontation and verbal attacks. Burr confronted Facebook's general council Colin Stretch about how Russians managed to pit Texans against each other for only $200 using Facebook.[2]

Networks of influencers, trolls, and bots, alongside carefully run ads and Facebook pages like Burr showed are common ways of controlling social media opinions. They're familiar to the social web: they're presences integral to how some governments manipulate their citizens and are similar to how some brands build their fan bases. And, they're easier than censorship. For an entity that doesn't own the network, or can't block access to it—which is generally the case when organizing protests in another country—manipulating the conversation using the right combination of personalities is easier.

How realistic the fake personalities in a campaign need to be depends on their target audience; some audiences are good at catching bots, while others don't do much digging. As such, armies of fake accounts that can be driven from anywhere in the world vary from cheap swarms of relatively unrealistic accounts that haven't existed for long, to more in-depth accounts that include phone numbers, profile pictures, and other elements to convince us that they're real people—there's plenty of content available online and it's hard to trace it. With some it can be hard, if not impossible, to tell them apart from a real person based on how they act in isolation.

Sophisticated bots are able to act like people on social

media: they write posts, and follow, like, and re-share other posts for the causes they support. The technology behind some bots can even understand the personalities of real social media users to better interact with them. At their most complex, bots stand in for brands or people and may even be able to talk with other users.

The use of these kinds of social media presences is expanding and has reached the political stage. This is worrisome because it's hard to discern the groups behind the personas involved in a campaign. Due to that difficulty and the ability to manipulate online conversation by influencing trending topics, we're entering a danger zone of manufactured conversation and artificially influenced views that even the U.S. government appears concerned about. Former FBI agent Clint Watts testified in early 2017 to the Senate Intelligence Committee about Russia's use of bots and trolls to plant false or misleading stories from sources of varying trustworthiness.[3]

But, realistic or not, online personas aren't effective without an audience—and in particular, an audience that trusts them. Often, they have one. In 2012, a study showed 30% of Twitter users could be fooled by a bot[4]. In 2016, *Adweek* reported Twitter's users trusted influencers almost as much as they trusted their friends.[5] That trust needed to come from somewhere.

Usually, it's a numbers game. Influencers tend to have large networks of followers, which can provide us with social proof. In other words, if that many other people trust them, could they be wrong? There are other factors as well which play with our psychology. Confirmation bias with repeated information, perceived friendliness, attractiveness, and our own perception that we're discerning about who we follow all play a role.[6]

However, influencers are loud and that type of presence doesn't fit every campaign need. Other social presences take a much quieter approach to gaining our trust. Some Russia-linked bots built trust by posing as local news outlets that were either fabricated or out of business, and posting only true stories.[7] The problem this poses is that bots that were doing this would largely be trusted by their audiences, since 82% of people have a high level of trust in their local news.[8] At any time, with the backing of an unknown entity, the bots could support any cause, true or not, and influence the surrounding narrative with their audiences trusting what they said.

While it may seem a bit far-fetched that bot armies could be manipulating us, it's already happening—and they're hard for us to catch.

In 2015, over 75,000 bots were used to dampen protests and fight critics of the Mexican government. The bots first appeared in 2012 and were used to disrupt hashtags being used to document human rights abuses, among other things, by spamming irrelevant content using the same tags.[9]

In a University of Southern California (USC) study, bots accounted for one fifth of political activity on Twitter in the 2016 U.S. election. Bots also accounted for 400,000 of the 2.8 million Twitter users that tweeted about the election, or about 15% of the users the USC study looked at. While bots supported candidates across the political spectrum, Mr. Trump had a significantly higher number of supporters that were bots rather than real people.[10] An army of these bots worked to spread fake news across the social web (and there are now online tools to see if you interacted with any).[11] On the 2016 election day, one group of known bots on Twitter promoted the hashtag "#WarAgainstDemocrats" more than 1,700 times.[12]

More recently, it was reported that bot armies were being used to beat down dissent against the Saudi Arabian government.[13] In one instance in 2018, an army of Russian bot accounts tweeted at the same time in to deny a Syrian gas attack—before the attack even happened.[14]

Bots hide so well that we don't know how many social media users are actually real, though we do know some platforms have a bigger bot presence than others. Ever-expanding numbers of bots contribute to an effect that *Forbes* contributor Michael Stone called "Bot Rot" in 2018,[15] a problem that appears to be getting worse. In summer 2017, a security researcher published a study which indicated that millions of Instagram users were actually bots.[16] The same year, Twitter shut down millions of bot accounts,[17] and it's suspected that 20-50% of the Twitter followers of some large personas, including Donald Trump, are bots,[18] though the effect of that isn't clear.

When bots act in unison, they're easier to track down. Research from cybersecurity company FireEye and an investigation by *The New York Times* turned up patterns that made bots identifiable when they were active. On both Twitter and Facebook, bots often posted the same or very similar messages in the alphabetical order of their names, suggesting software running through a list of bot accounts. Not all their messages spread across the social ecosystem but some did, which was enough to trigger anger and paranoia in an already polarized political system.

In 2018, the U.S. Department of Justice indicted three Russian companies and thirteen Russian individuals for interfering in the 2016 election. The Russian efforts included creating fake accounts on social media sites and posting comments. A former employee of one implicated troll farm told *TIME* that the most frequent targets to spread disinformation about in 2014 were then-President Barack Obama and German Chancellor Angela Merkel,[19] though the Department of Justice described a broader propaganda effort.

> The Department of Justice announced that a grand jury in the District of Columbia today returned an indictment presented by the Special Counsel's Office. The indictment charges

thirteen Russian nationals and three Russian companies for committing federal crimes while seeking to interfere in the United States political system, including the 2016 Presidential election. The defendants allegedly conducted what they called "information warfare against the United States," with the stated goal of "spread[ing] distrust towards the candidates and the political system in general."[20]

While the Department of Justice deals with the bot and troll problem from a judicial perspective, social sites are searching for their own solutions. The search has not been going smoothy. Tumblr's trouble with handling bots and illegal content on its platform became widely known when it decided to ban adult content. Twitter has internally acknowledged possible legal problems with taking down troll and bot accounts as well as the business implications of culling its slow-growing userbase.[21] Questionable presences have been a part of Twitter nearly since its beginnings and the site has yet to find a solution for them, something then chief-executive Dick Costolo acknowledged in a 2015 company memo.

We suck at dealing with abuse and trolls on the platform and we've sucked at it for years.[22]

The bot problem is likely to get worse as bots grow more complex and as bigger actors invest in them. In 2011, the United States Central Command awarded a contract for an "online persona management service" which included fake online profiles to a firm in California—effectively a bot army—so we know even state actors in democratic countries have taken an interest.[23] While the U.S. Central Command may be investing in its own answer to social media bots, bot armies are easily available to anyone who knows where to look for them. *The Daily Beast* bought access to an army of 1,000 accounts for just $45 and found they could buy software to control it for another $250.[24] Bot armies are advertised for anywhere from what *The Daily Beast* spent to more for armies of accounts that have existed longer or otherwise seem to be more legitimate.

Although social networks are actively fighting the problem, bots and trolls continue to thrive. In May and June 2018, Twitter suspended 70 million fake and suspicious accounts and continued the same pace into July. Despite the take-downs, bots were still active across social media, spreading similar political messages. Faced with the possibility of a "Blue Wave" in the 2018 midterm election, bot activity ramped back up, and developed campaigns to discourage the Democratic vote.

One campaign, "#WalkAway," made it to the top of Twitter's hashtags. "#WalkAway" was a hashtag posted from accounts that claimed to be leaving the Democratic party because they were offended by Democratic "intolerance and incivility".[25] It was recognized by *Fox News* as a grassroots movement, but the accounts behind the tweets were largely identified as bots. One tweet, retweeted over 16,000 times, read:

> Both my parents are Hispanic LEGAL
> immigrants, both were registered Democrats,
> and both this week told me they have decided to
> #WalkAway[26]

The account that posted it was not a real person. Twitter suspended the account after users discovered the account had a profile picture photoshopped from a face on the cover of a book about penny stocks and did not appear to have a credible history.

Influencers and trolls joined the bot armies to push similar messages. Another account, this time a right-wing influencer, tweeted:

> The Democratic Party is the party of slavery.
> The party of Jim Crow. The party of segregation.
> The party of the KKK.
>
> Democrats walked away from black folks long
> ago. Now, it's our time to #WalkAway.[27]

The person behind the tweet had been famous on various right-wing sites for a while, helped campaign for Texas Republican Senator Ted Cruz, and had published viral stunts targeting former president Barack Obama.[28] Given their background, the individual was clearly not a recent convert who was walking away from the Democratic party. But, the algorithms didn't know, and the tweets added to the activity pushing the #WalkAway campaign to the top of the list.

And, that's part of the problem. With a big enough campaign, anything can go viral. Whether it's 3,000 Facebook ads, influencers in a viral Twitter campaign, or an army of bots, we should be concerned with what the social trends and presences we encounter actually are. Though some are completely legitimate, others might be backed by unknown groups that intend to steer our discussions for reasons that aren't always apparent. As former Deputy Attorney General Rod J. Rosenstein said after the indictment of thirteen Russian individuals and three companies, "This indictment serves as a reminder that people are not always who they appear to be on the Internet."[29]

7 · THE PROPAGANDISTS

> It is not possible to apply censorship to this
> enormous amount of data. Thus censorship is
> not the correct word choice. But no censorship
> does not mean no management—China State
> Internet Information Office[1]

In 1993, John Gilmore, a founder of the Electronic
Frontier Foundation, explained why censorship of the
Internet is so difficult: "The Net interprets censorship as
damage and routes around it."[2] Though Gilmore's
explanation came in 1993, it has generally held true. A
dedicated person can almost always access blocked
content. But, that's when a ban works as intended.
Banning information outright, or trying to intimidate
people out of sharing it, doesn't work predictably.
Doing so risks backlash or the "Streisand effect" where
attempts to hide information draw more attention to it.

The other problem with controlling the web is the
deluge of data. China's online citizens were generating

thirty billion pieces of information every day as of 2015.[3] A massive amount of information far too large for traditional censorship to counter, yet China is a country at the forefront of a censored web. Faced with the deluge of information, a former director of China's state information office recognized the challenge and said the country had it under control using means other than direct censorship—no censorship didn't mean no management.

The modern way of censoring the Internet embraces the flow of information and steers the conversation using armies of accounts. It's referred to as "flooding" and involves creating a torrent of information, some accurate, some fake, and some biased, to overwhelm us. Social media makes flooding easy—pushing a topic viral can involve inexpensive armies of bot accounts and influencers. Information doesn't need to be believable, it just needs to be widely shared. Rather than generating backlash, flooding creates confusion and noise, making it hard to know what, if anything, can be trusted.

Regardless of the entity behind a flooding campaign and its intended targets, the rest of us are not immune. The global and public nature of popular social media make those networks prime targets for torrents of disinformation from governments trying to control the dialogue. At the same time, it's impossible for the effects to stay within the borders of countries trying to keep their citizens in line.

In some cases, leaking propaganda is intentional; a foreign actor might intend to attack citizens of another country to weaken its institutions by sowing fear and doubt. It's a scorched-earth approach where the goal is to create doubt, break faith in institutions that should otherwise be trustworthy, and manipulate politics with the resulting paranoia. We lose track of what's true, start to question everything, and eventually refuse to believe anything at all. Some countries, including the U.S., are cautious about leaking propaganda to their own citizens, so they don't use social media for offensive action that might help defend us.

> "If you blip out enough false stories, then people just switch off ultimately. They end up not knowing what's true, and they end up not believing anything," Ben Nimmo, an international security analyst and former NATO press officer dealing with Russia and Ukraine, explained to *U.S. News*. "There's this kind of informational nihilism to coin a phrase. It's a destruction of the belief that there is any such thing as a reliable source."[4]

Foreign-backed online disinformation campaigns have been widespread and growing, taking the form of Facebook pages, ads, leaked emails, and other digital content. All major social networks have reported they have removed millions of accounts involved in disinformation. The campaigns aren't limited in effect to the Internet, though they spread most quickly through social networks. Russia-backed groups have launched protests and counter protests in real life, everything from rallies in support of LGBTQ+ causes to rallies in support of the 2nd Amendment. In summer 2017, two different Russia-backed Facebook pages organized dueling rallies in Texas in the same location with neither rally aware of its counterpart until the day of. Although Russia has frequently been in the news for its targeting of the 2016 U.S. election, China, Israel, ISIS, and fringe groups on the far left and right sides of the U.S. political spectrum have also run various targeted campaigns,[5] although their strategies are sometimes very different.

Russia's disinformation strategy is effective, but is intended to be difficult to uncover. There is no "Russian" brand for online propaganda (official Russian news outlets like *Sputnik* notwithstanding). Instead, it's designed to build trust and blend in to the rest of the conversation, while surreptitiously disrupting it with manufactured crowds. Fake accounts that looked real at a glance made comments, pushed content into the trending topics on sites, and reached mainstream audiences by posing as local news. It was a guerrilla propaganda technique that was hard to catch because it was based on building trust first and misinforming later. *NPR* noted from one investigation that 48 fake Twitter accounts were discovered posing as local news, including names like @Seattle_Post, @ElPasoTopNews, and @MilwaukeeVoice.[6] Bret Schafer, a social media analyst with the Alliance for Securing Democracy discussed the accounts with *NPR*.

> They set them up for a reason. And if at any given moment, they wanted to operationalize this network of what seemed to be local American news handles, they can significantly influence the narrative on a breaking news story. But now instead of just showing up online and flooding it with news sites, they have these accounts with two years of credible history.[7]

Sometimes, propaganda campaigns play with our trust by exploiting our emotions. Interest targeting makes it worse, because propaganda can be targeted to exactly the people who need to see it. It spreads because it confirms our beliefs and makes us feel strongly about them. In 2017, this style of propaganda from a Russia-backed Facebook page, Blacktivists, caught Black Lives Matter activists. The page posted videos of police brutality—in the hope of attracting people whose Facebook targeting data said were suspicious of police and concerned about civil rights. In another case, Republican voters were targeted by a Twitter account that claimed to be the "unofficial account of the Tennessee Republican party," @GOP_TEN. @GOP_TEN posted fake news including false claims of voter fraud in Florida, and was often retweeted by Donald Trump Jr. and Trump aide Kellyanne Conway.[8]

It's tactics like these that make the recently popularized term "fake news" so dangerous. While the term is intended to describe disinformation or misinformation posing as news, it has been co-opted as an accusation against legitimate news that people simply disagree with. "#FakeNews" is a widely-used social hashtag promoted by everyone from Donald Trump to Kremlin-linked bots—in campaigns that themselves resemble, and sometimes are, fake news.

That's not to discount the fact that that fake news and biased news are very real problems. Unfortunately, the accusations of them have lost much of their meaning because of the political motivations behind them. Some will look for any reason, valid or not, to accuse a news network of being fake.

The full effect of campaigns to accuse legitimate news as being fake has lead to confusion across social media, where truly fake news is lumped together with factual news accused of being fake news because we disagreed with it, and an increasing distrust in the media. We've taken a serious accusation and turned it into something political and almost meaningless at the same time fake news and propaganda have been growing into real and dangerous problems.

Other groups, such as ISIS, manipulate social media to spread propaganda more directly. Using the features of social platforms as designed, ISIS found ways to game the system and magnify messages it wanted to spread, earning it the nickname "The World's Deadliest Tech Startup" from *Vanity Fair* in 2016.[9] ISIS has a distinct social media brand to rival the best, with consistent styles, color schemes, and iconography.[10]

Put another way, the group isn't hiding—ISIS is the opposite of Russian propaganda. The group is proud to be known on social media and wants us to be able to find its content. ISIS has presences on nearly every social network and chat service, and uses them to spread propaganda more effectively than some tech startups manage to market themselves. The group shares footage of beheadings on YouTube, videos that are even more gruesome on LiveLeak, and uses Internet Radio to constantly reach followers.[11] When a terror attack happens, the group takes credit on Twitter in front of a crowd of cheering Twitter followers.

The actual size of ISIS is unknown, with estimates ranging from under 10,000 involved individuals to over 200,000, depending on the year and the source of the estimate. On social media, they make a good show of being larger-than-life. We don't know how many ISIS-linked Twitter accounts belong to real people as opposed to bot networks run by the group. The group's messaging gets an even wider reach from users of the official ISIS Twitter Android app, which sends tweets—complete with hashtags, links, and images—from the accounts of people who have installed and signed up for the service. Tweet campaigns via the app are staggered to avoid Twitter's spam filters taking issue with hundreds of users tweeting the same content at the same time.[12] Due to the loyalty of these followers, ISIS doesn't need to spend as much effort building fake personalities because real people are willing to help.

With the help of its app, ISIS-run Twitter campaigns have been quite successful and have allowed ISIS to, among other things, control the results for certain searches. During the group's march on Mosul, Iraq in 2014, almost 40,000 tweets were posted in a single day via the ISIS app. ISIS was promoting an image of an armed jihadist looking at the ISIS flag flying over the city with the text "We are coming, Baghdad." The volume of tweets was enough to impact Twitter's search algorithms, and caused any search for "Baghdad" to show the image among the top results.[13]

Social networks have been carefully walking the line of censorship and their promises free speech when it comes to online propaganda and fake news, while we grapple with the problems ourselves. Along with the millions of fake accounts already taken down, sites have been responsive to investigations like the one that turned up fake local news accounts. Twitter has been removing masses of bot accounts that were traced to Russia, and all social networks have been trying to take down extremist content when it appears. Neither approach has solved the problem. Each time, various voices have pushed back with warnings about censorship, but public opinion appears to be changing.

But, while some countries launch offensives on social media, others haven't figured out how to fight back. In the U.S., the government is in a hard place when it comes to social media propaganda offensives. U.S. law prevents the intelligence community from fighting back with social media campaigns of its own because U.S. citizens might see the same propaganda. The U.S. Department of Defense gets caught in the same regulations—though sometimes incorrectly because it has different objectives. The law was written with print, radio, and TV in mind—and its protections are important, but also make it much harder to go on the offensive in wider reaching spaces like the Internet. Other laws, which protect our privacy, restrict investigations into the groups behind propaganda campaigns by categorizing such investigations under intelligence collection which adds bureaucracy.[14]

Those laws have been used against United States operations. In March 2006, a U.S. Special Forces Soldiers battalion and an Iraqi Special Forces unit ran a successful operation against a Jaish al-Mahdi death squad. Less than an hour after the operation, someone rearranged the scene, removed the guns to make it look like death squad soldiers had been killed at prayer, and posted photos online alleging an atrocity. Though the U.S. had video proof of what happened during the operation, the propaganda effort was successful—it was picked up by both Arab and U.S. news networks. Due to U.S. laws the military waited 3 days before attempting an unsuccessful social media defense. The battalion was forced out of commission for a month long investigation.[15]

When propaganda efforts can take a successful battalion out of commission, we realize how big the capabilities of those trying to manage our online dialog are—and how much more powerful it can be than simple censorship. There isn't a unified fight against extremism and disinformation campaigns, and the various social platforms we use don't appear to be working to change that. But, that doesn't change the fact that our social media appears to be circulating propaganda that's easy for us to fall for. We don't fully understand where it is or where it will come from so neither social media nor ourselves are well-equipped to deal with it.

8 · THE FINDERS

> The case raises the question of whether the
> First Amendment protects as speech the
> results produced by an Internet search engine.
> The Court concludes that, at least in the
> circumstances presented here, it does.
> Accordingly, allowing Plaintiffs to sue Baidu
> for what are in essence editorial judgments
> about which political ideas to promote would
> run afoul of the First Amendment.[1]

In 2014, a San Francisco court ruled that the way Baidu, a Chinese search engine, orders its search results was protected by the company's First Amendment rights.[2] The ruling was wide reaching. Of the 5 billion search queries per day Baidu serviced in 2013,[3] and the 5.5 billion daily Google searches in 2016[4]—numbers which are much higher now and not to mention other search engines, the companies involved were within their rights to order their search results however they saw fit.

Although the court ruling was a win for search companies, it wasn't bad news for the rest of us—it ensured that the reasons we use the search engines we choose would stay. The order of search results is one factor that distinguishes search engines from each other.

But, there's a bad side to search rankings. Even with the best intentions different algorithms produce different results, with potentially different biases. This is why, for example, some search engines have a reputation for being good at finding porn while others have a reputation for being good at finding programming resources. It also makes it possible to game search results by targeting searches based on their specific wording without any bias from the search engine itself. In the case where the search engine is the dominant one (Google, for example, has 67% of U.S. searches[4]), dropping a site's search ranking can make it almost disappear.

And, some websites have nearly disappeared at the hands of search giants. Foundem, a comparison-shopping search engine launched in 2005 by UK entrepreneur couple Shivaun and Adam Raff, competed with Google in the search space. For reasons they couldn't determine, their search service was penalized by Google—Google's word for dropping a site's rankings. Foundem effectively disappeared from the Internet for Google users between 2006 and 2009. Adam Raff made his support for search neutrality clear in the wake of his battle with Google.

> Without search neutrality rules to constrain
> Google's competitive advantage, we may be
> heading toward a bleakly uniform world of
> Google Everything — Google Travel, Google
> Finance, Google Insurance, Google Real Estate,
> Google Telecoms and, of course, Google Books.[5]

Search companies carefully guard their algorithms as proprietary technology. The best information we get about them is clues about how they rank websites. Google says that in addition to relevancy, mobile-friendliness and HTTPS availability factored into a site's search rankings. Amazon told sellers that how often their products were purchased factored in, followed by keywords, "Fulfilled by Amazon," then product reviews. Bing published a list of guidelines that focused on content, links to a site, social media, and page load time, among other factors. A website could improve its search ranking by following the suggestions of search providers, but it wasn't a guarantee because there are other, unpublished factors that influence rankings.

It's the unpublished factors that can hurt us most, and we can only guess at what they are. Google has been involved in multiple lawsuits over low rankings or even blacklisting of sites and competitors.[6] Facebook and Amazon have both been accused of manipulating results due to influence from paying companies or to target results to users. While most search providers promise neutrality, their algorithms may not be as neutral as they intend. Engineers who design and build the software that powers search engines can unintentionally build their personal biases into the system.

Often, it's hard to tell until those algorithms are in use and then, only if certain patterns develop. In early 2017, Amazon scrapped an internal AI-based recruiting tool that was under development since 2014. The tool turned out to be sexist—which was a problem it was trying to eliminate. The reason for building the tool was to eliminate such biases from the company's hiring process.[7] When asked about Amazon's AI recruiting tool, Nihar Shah, a professor of machine learning at Carnegie Mellon University, told *CNBC* that "how to ensure that the algorithm is fair, how to make sure the algorithm is really interpretable and explainable—that's still quite far off."[8]

The fact that we don't know the biases that the algorithms might have isn't lost on those who aren't in the technology community. Republican politicians have accused Google of favoring liberal views in its search results, going so far as to call Google CEO Sundar Pichai to testify to Congress. Representative Matt Gaetz from Florida asked "how can I have confidence that you're protecting the sanctity of your system when you don't even know your employees are getting together on your own company's infrastructure to talk about political activity?"[9] in reference to leaked employee emails about classifying *Breitbart* content as hate speech. Pichai responded that Google was built to be resilient to such issues. Representative Ted Lieu from California suggested that the problem wasn't Google. "If you want positive searches, do positive things. If you get bad press, don't blame Google. Consider blaming yourself."[10] Google does, however, have the ability to make changes and corrections to its search and search suggestions in processes unknown to us.

Robert Epstein, a researcher from the American Institute for Behavioral Research and Technology, has been studying Google's search in hopes of revealing what lays behind the curtain. He believed Google had the ability to manipulate elections through its search results. Epstein ran experiments that showed biased rankings could influence the opinions of independent voters. He noted that part of Google's search rankings had to do with how often other sites linked to a page, how many visitors a site got, and how often a page was updated. Epstein explained to *The Guardian* that those factors could give an advantage to more extreme views, which tend to be published and updated more actively than other content.

> These two manipulations can work together to have an enormous impact on people without their knowledge that they are being manipulated, and our research shows that very clearly. Virtually no one is aware of bias in search suggestions or rankings.[11]

Search engines typically try to stay relatively neutral, and can overcompensate when accused of bias. Shortly after Epstein released research indicating Google was suppressing negative news about presidential candidate Hillary Clinton during the 2016 election cycle in the United States, Google appeared to adjust its algorithms. In doing so, the search giant may have been too heavy-handed. Epstein noticed that after those changes, a flood of pro-Trump and anti-Clinton search results, including fake news, appeared in searches more often and ranked higher—which he made clear was not his intent. "If I had to do it over again I would not have released those data. There is some indication that they had an impact that was detrimental to Hillary Clinton, which was never my intention."[12]

Not everyone drew the same conclusion as Epstein. Instead, they said that partisan websites—primarily right-wing ones—were better at optimizing themselves for higher rankings. By popularizing terms like "cuckservative" and rallying cries like "feminism is cancer," they could make search algorithms better rank their sites for searches that related to those terms. Shane Burley, a journalist and "alt-right" researcher told *The Guardian* "it has this effect of making certain words kind of like magic words in search algorithms."[13]

Skewing search results by popularizing terms is nothing new. Reputation management services and marketers have been doing it for a long time—and so have extremists. Something that is new is online communities learning strategies to do the same thing using social media. Redditors have been dropping so-called "Google bombs" to influence Google Image results, an action that Reddit's administrators frown on but have little power to stop. Users craft large numbers of posts with carefully chosen keywords that they know Google will pick up. The strategy has pushed photos of Donald Trump into the top results for both "45th President" and "idiot", and CNN's logo to the top results for "fake news." Similar battles have pushed photos of Donald Trump and Bill Clinton—by left and right leaning communities, respectively—into the top results for "Rapist" (in addition to other graphic results).[14]

"The key has traditionally been connected to influencing the algorithm with a high volume of biased search terms" Brittan Heller, director of society and technology at the Anti-Defamation League told *The Guardian*.[15]

Similar strategies influence auto-complete when we start typing in the search bar. Based on what exactly we type, our suggestions and results may be very different from what someone else sees, skewed in a particular ideological direction if not an entirely false direction—even if we're searching for the same thing. Search suggestions have no promise of neutrality—some are targeted to us and others are based on common searches. How they're generated allows websites to manipulate the suggestions we might see by using the same wording they expect we would.

Certain media outlets—once again primarily

conservative ones and fake news, according to observations from a study—have learned to anticipate what their audiences will search for and the language they'll use when looking for it. Using that information, they can manipulate the feature to push searchers towards their content,[16] just as they do to improve their search rankings. Those tactics could work across the political spectrum.

Other times, search algorithms simply get things wrong. Google Search shows what Google calls "instant answers" when its search engine is sure it has a direct answer to a question, and it has made some strange claims. Among other things, instant answers have suggested that the Republican party was a group of Nazis and that Barack Obama was planning a coup d'état.[17] To Google's credit, it takes wrong instant answers seriously and provides tools for users to report them and makes manual corrections. Although we've come to believe that the top-rated search results and instant answers are the most correct answers, there's no guarantee.

Concern about the direction search seems to be moving in has created a new industry of alternative search engines. They promise neutral, transparent, and privacy-respecting alternatives to the well-known search giants. Though they don't operate on the scale of billions of searches per day, they have active and outspoken communities. One, DuckDuckGo, saw an average of 30 million searches per day in 2018—more than AOL, but representing a market share of only 0.18%.[18]

Gabriel Weinberg, founder and CEO of DuckDuckGo, explained concerns about targeted and biased search results in response to a question on Quora, a question and answer site.

> That may appear at first blush to be a good thing, but when most people say they want personalization in a search context they actually want localization. They want local weather and restaurants, which can actually be provided without tracking, like we do at DuckDuckGo. That's because approximate location info is automatically embedded by your computer in the search request, which we can use to serve you local results and immediately throw away without tracking you.
>
> Beyond localization, personalized results are dangerous because to show you results they think you'll click on, they must filter results they think you'll skip. That's why it's called the Filter Bubble.
>
> So if you have political leanings one way or another, you're more likely to get results you already agree with, and less likely to ever see opposing viewpoints. In the aggregate this leads to increased echo chambers that are significantly contributing to our increasingly polarized

society.[19]

Even though not all alternative search options are transparent enough to give searchers the option to understand why they see the results they get, they're a step in the right direction. Their communities are interested in making their services better and less biased. Some are even completely open about their technology. With the expanding reach of search engines, how and why results are ranked matters. But, we're not at a point where search engines—even many of the alternative ones—give us the transparency we need. Until they do, we're right to sometimes be suspicious about our search results. Frank Pasquale, a law professor from the University of Maryland, told *CNET* that without transparency there was no end in sight for the suspicions around search engine secrets.

> When it comes to political bias, the lack of
> transparency and the lack of ability for the
> public to understand how it works, means
> suspicion will continue.[20]

Our need for search transparency is growing alongside the fake news that's taking over our Internet. Search algorithms can and do fall for lies and fake news, even occasionally surfacing them as designated answers to searches—and they will continue to. Extremists, marketers, and propagandists have been manipulating rankings for a long time. Since fake news tends to spread faster than truth, it can get picked up by search algorithms that assume it's just as trustworthy as real news. We don't know when or why that happens because our search engines haven't given us the tools to protect ourselves.

THE CAPTORS

9 · THE TRACKERS

> "We knew that if we could identify them in their second trimester, there's a good chance we could capture them for years," Pole told me. "As soon as we get them buying diapers from us, they're going to start buying everything else too. If you're rushing through the store, looking for bottles, and you pass orange juice, you'll grab a carton. Oh, and there's that new DVD I want. Soon, you'll be buying cereal and paper towels from us, and keep coming back."[1]

Andrew Pole, a statistician at Target, was approached in 2002 by Target's marketing department which wanted the answer to an important question in retail. Would it be possible, they wondered, to figure out if a customer was pregnant even if that customer didn't want them to know.[2] The question was important because the retail chain hoped to convince new parents to buy everything they needed there—after all, the stores carry everything from food to lawn furniture—by sending new parents coupons when their shopping habits were most likely to change after a new baby. The marketing department hoped to reach those potential new customers before competition did.

Pole was, as an often-told story says, successful at answering their question. About a year after he created a pregnancy prediction model, a Minneapolis man walked into a Target demanding to speak to a manager about a mailer addressed to his high school aged daughter. In it were advertisements for maternity clothes and nursery supplies. A manager offered an apology for sending maternity advertisements to a high school student. However, Target's predictions were correct.[3]

"My daughter got this in the mail!" he said. "She's still in high school, and you're sending her coupons for baby clothes and cribs? Are you trying to encourage her to get pregnant?"

The manager didn't have any idea what the man was talking about. He looked at the mailer. Sure enough, it was addressed to the man's daughter and contained advertisements for maternity clothing, nursery furniture and pictures of smiling infants. The manager apologized and then called a few days later to apologize again.

On the phone, though, the father was somewhat

abashed. "I had a talk with my daughter," he said. "It turns out there's been some activities in my house I haven't been completely aware of. She's due in August. I owe you an apology."[4]

There is a chance, of course, that the incident was a coincidence. It's possible that the daughter had been placed in the wrong marketing category by accident. Target itself acknowledged that customers might not want it to know if they were pregnant and might not send coupons that were as blatant as the story suggests —and which would therefore be unlikely to arouse suspicion.

Whether the story is completely true or not, Target's tracking information pales in comparison to what the web provides today. The information gathered by online tracking services is something Pole probably couldn't even have dreamed of in 2002. Our smartphones get us online anytime, anywhere, and services are watching. Virtual assistants figure out our habits to remember where we parked, to remind us to use our loyalty cards when we go shopping, and to tell us about the traffic before we leave for work. Other services live quietly in the shadows, gathering information about where we visit and how long we stay —online and off.

The data isn't always accurate, but it's generally good enough to be effective or, at least, good enough for advertisers to pay for it. It allows advertisers to put ads in front of the people who are most likely to click on them. Though the data may be imperfect, it increases clicks enough that the data is still valuable. A reporter from *The Atlantic* purchased her data from a data broker in 2017 and found it to be about 50% accurate.[5] I found similar results after using a now defunct browser extension called Data Selfie to try to deduce my personality based on my Facebook activity. The data was occasionally correct (I'm a male who likes dogs and net neutrality), but generally a little inaccurate unless my gym visits are a lie and I hate going outside.

That tracking data gives us the convenience features and personalized recommendations we've come to expect, but also powers the targeted ads we see across the web. It gives ad services, such as Google's AdWords, Facebook, Amazon, and others the ability to know us even if we don't have an account on their services—Facebook calls these "shadow profiles." Much of this tracking is invisible to us, even though it does quite a bit to pick apart our privacy to show relevant content. Depending on our perspective, this does some variation of improving our online experience or invading our privacy. The developers of ad-blocking browser extension uBlock Origin take the position that ads are a privacy invasion.

> Ads, "unintrusive" or not, are just the visible portions of privacy-invading apparatus entering your browser when you visit most sites nowadays.[6]

We're generally accustomed to being targeted based on

our demographics or behaviors, which are about who we are and what we do. Demographic information includes our sex and gender, age, income, and family— the things which are easy for targeting systems to ask for. Behavior information is about what we buy and what we use. But, there's a new depth of targeting rolling out to advertisers: psychographic. Psychographic traits are much more personal—they're about our motivations. Things like our fears, our values, what we find fulfilling, and our personal goals. Based on our online behavior, the services we use can surmise some of our psychographic traits even down to things we don't realize about ourselves.

This is different from the targeting of other mediums. With, for example, a TV ad, there's no guarantee that the intended audience for an ad will see it. Rather, the ad would generally be shown on the channels where its target audience would most likely be—but it would still reach a wide audience. With an online ad, the ad can reach an extremely specific audience, or even a single individual without anyone else knowing. The data that powers them can be very specific and personal. For some sites, targeting information is used to decide much more; not only do we see ads chosen specifically for us, but content chosen specifically for us.

Ads and content that are targeted to us can influence the way we think and the way we see ourselves, even if we're not directly interested in what the ad is selling. A 2016 study revealed that ads changed participants' perceptions of themselves based on the content of the ad and whether they were led to believe the ad was targeted. Researchers showed participants an ad for a high-end watch brand, telling some that the ad was targeted, and others that the ad was not. Participants were asked to rate themselves on a sophistication scale, and those who believed the ad was targeted rated themselves higher.[7]

The researchers did a similar experiment, this time showing participants a targeted ad for an environmentally friendly product. Not only did the participants rate themselves more "green" and more willing to buy the product, but they were also more willing to donate to an environmental charity.[8] The effect was only studied in the short term, during the same lab session, so there is no data from this study about any potential longer-term effects on our perception of ourselves.

The targeting of the ads needed to be at least moderately accurate to work—that is, it needed to be plausibly connected to past behavior. Otherwise, the ads did not increase the likelihood of viewers buying and did not lead to any apparent changes in how viewers perceived themselves. The ads in the study were not directly targeted to the participants—the researchers only created the perception that they were —but it was enough to have an effect. Online, where ads truly are targeted, the effects may be more pronounced.[9]

Sometimes though, the opposite can be true. The *Harvard Business Review* found that if people disliked how their information was being shared by a platform, their interest in purchasing a product dropped when they were shown an ad for it on that platform. The same was true for political ads. Almost two-thirds of people surveyed in 2012 said they would be less likely to vote for a political candidate if they found out that candidate was targeting advertisements to them by buying information about what they did online.[10] In the same study, 86% of Americans said they did not want political ads targeted to them based on their interests.

Although we might not care that ads might influence us to buy something—after all, that is their purpose—it does raise concerns when it might influence us to vote for something. Even though the general opinion is against it, political ads are also targeted. It's nothing new, but online advertising made the targeting much more personal. Robert Epstein, who has studied bias in Google Search, told *The Guardian* of similar concerns.

> This gives companies like Google even more power to influence people's opinions, attitudes, beliefs and behaviors.[11]

In recent elections and referendums such as the 2016 U.S. election and Brexit, we've seen a new form of ads being used to manipulate voters based on very specific psychographic traits. Ads targeted in this way have been called "dark ads," and were run by firms including Cambridge Analytica and AggregateIQ.[12]

Dark ads are aimed very specifically at certain psychographic traits, and in some cases if a group outside the targeted group were to see them, it could be a problem for the ad campaign's effectiveness. When they work, however, they're effective at swinging political opinions. They make it possible for advertising campaigns to appeal to our worst aspects, things we may not even realize about ourselves.

In general, we tend to see more concern about dark ads from the "losing" side, but they should worry us even if they helped us "win." That's because even if we got our way, the fact that it was what we wanted might not have been up to us—or even good for us. They may also work against us—that is, to support something we don't—the next time. Chris Sumner, research director and co-founder of the Online Privacy Foundation and leader of dark ad research, presented concerns about the manipulating effects of dark ads at Def Con in 2017.

> Before the [Brexit] referendum results, the concern we had was that people's biases were being manipulated, either intentionally or unintentionally. Now we've seen this [research], I'm as concerned as I was before.

> It's not a surprise, it's what we expected to see. People on one side, whichever side happens to be winning at the time, are going to say 'no, it's not a problem', while people who have just lost are going to see it as a big problem.[13]

Dark ads tend to fall well within the filter bubbles of the people who see them. Ads that are highly emotional but also highly targeted can lead to communities or even entire nations of people who are angry about things nobody else even knows about. We're more likely to engage with the ads or headlines that make us feel strong (particularly if they make us angry)[14], and the fact that we engaged with them means we'll see more of them.

Whether these types of specifically targeted ads should be allowed in politics is a question we're facing right now. Although dark ad firms have recently been involved, that may change. The data Cambridge Analytica used to target voters, and new Facebook features that allowed psychographic targeting are relatively recent, but will become more available to advertisers. As retailers and other ad firms learn to use the targeting more effectively, the ads they run will get more effective and more manipulative.

Many ad platforms don't offer transparency into the source of an ad; they just run the ad and charge the entity behind it accordingly. Whether the ad is from a foreign actor, a local political campaign, or a random individual with spare money is hard to know. Federal ad transparency regulations that require advertisers to disclose who or what paid for a political ad in other mediums don't really apply to online ads.[15]

Since online ads are so targeted, there may not be a lot of people who see an ad, let alone a lot of people who are interested in questioning it or demanding transparency. In particular, online advertising platforms are not well-equipped to handle political ads with the transparency and accountability that's needed, especially with highly psychographically targeted advertisements. Phil Weisner, a professor of law and telecommunications at the University of Colorado, discussed the issue with *Marketplace*.

> You have to offer the best available rate for political advertising, that has to be done in a very transparent and equal fashion. With respect to Facebook, there's no transparency. And we don't really know what sorts of ranges are being made. Who is buying the ads? How much they're paying? That's now being debated in Congress. Mark Warner, for example, has a bill saying that Facebook should be subject to some of the same rules that happens on TV. So the political ads are transparent and that they're also fair, in terms of who has to pay how much.[16]

Advertising platforms are trying to improve transparency with better labeling but there's still work to do. Facebook rolled out an experimental policy in Canada in late 2017 that required all advertisers to have a Facebook page, and on that page allowed people outside an ad's targeted group to see the ad. While this was an improvement over what Facebook had, it was imperfect and fell short of what critics pushed for. Ads were only available temporarily and could be hard to find.[17] In some cases, the labels that showed who backed an ad weren't reliable and could even be misleading.

Under the experimental transparency policy, Airbnb ran ads opposing rental restrictions in Toronto. However, Airbnb did not directly run the ads; instead, it used its marketing and public policy arm, Airbnb Citizen. Airbnb Citizen described itself as a "community of hosts, guests and other believers in the power of home sharing to help tackle economic, environmental and social challenges around the world," a tagline that made it sound like a community organization. Though the ads were from Airbnb, it was hard for the average person to trace them back. The company told *ProPublica* it was clear about its ties to Airnbnb Citizen, but Facebook's experimental feature didn't make it obvious.[18]

Advertising platforms have also struggled to verify who is actually behind an ad. *VICE News* demonstrated flaws in Facebook's ad labeling by buying Facebook ads pretending to be "Paid for by" all 100 U.S. senators, Vice President Mike Pence, and ISIS in late 2018. Facebook approved all the ads.

> To test it, VICE News applied to buy fake ads on behalf of all 100 sitting U.S. senators, including ads "Paid for by" by Mitch McConnell and Chuck Schumer. Facebook's approvals were bipartisan: All 100 sailed through the system, indicating that just about anyone can buy an ad

identified as "Paid for by" by a major U.S. politician.[19]

Until ad platforms and regulations catch up, ads will get smarter targeting that slips deeper into our filter bubbles, tailored increasingly to our internal beliefs with little transparency. Our feeds and our ads will get increasingly manipulative. If we don't know who paid for an ad and why we saw it, firms like Cambridge Analytica can continue to create ad-based realities by manipulating our emotions. Target might know when we're pregnant, but dark ads know our fears even when we don't realize them ourselves—and they're not just sending coupons.

10 · THE FAKERS

Looking back at the video, it does not in fact show Acosta "placing his hands" on the woman. But about 90 minutes after she posted her string of tweets, Infowars editor Paul Joseph Watson tweeted out a video of the incident that was doctored to make it look like Acosta chopped the woman's arm with his hand.

[...]

Comparing the actual footage of the news conference with the Watson/Sanders videos clearly shows that the latter has been manipulated.[1]

Former White House Press Secretary Sarah Sanders promoted a doctored video as evidence against *CNN*'s Jim Acosta in 2018, to support banning him from press briefings. With an obviously doctored video, some seemed to be counting on our gullibility. They were right, we are gullible. It's hard for us to figure out when we're presented with fake photo, video, or audio evidence. In a 2017 study of 700 people, participants were able to tell when a picture had been manipulated only slightly better than if they guessed at random (about 60% were able to identify a fake). Of the ones who were able to identify manipulated images, fewer than half could tell what in the image had been changed.[2] Jill Nightingale, an author of the study, told *The Washington Post* her thoughts about the study's findings:

> It's a bit worrying. Photos are incredibly
> powerful. They influence how we see the world.
> They can even influence our memory of things.
> If we can't tell the fake ones from the real ones,
> the fakes are going to be powerful, too.[3]

Not only are the fakes powerful, they're getting better. With quality image manipulation software, spreading convincing hoax images is getting easier and catching those hoaxes is getting harder. Sound and video can now be spoofed as well and the Internet has already adopted the software behind those spoofs as its new toys. Technology for audio and video manipulation and creation is still young and has mainly showed up in technology demonstrations and research projects, but some of it is available for free. The results are far more convincing than changing the speed of a video to manufacture inappropriate behavior.

In 2016, a computer graphics, machine learning, and computer vision research group published a paper about an application they created called Face2Face. The researchers demonstrated Face2Face by creating extensive fake footage of various political figures mimicking the facial expressions of an actor.[4]

In July 2017, University of Washington researchers posted an eight-minute video to YouTube of former president Barack Obama speaking. The video, aside from the audio which could have been sourced from anywhere, is fake. It was created by feeding tens of hours of speeches from Obama into an AI system then using the system to generate the video.[5] In it, Obama's lips are correctly synchronized with the speech, and it's extremely difficult to pinpoint the video as a fake. The legitimate use of these kinds of software is filmmaking and CGI to allow for more realistic animation, but the possibility for fake news and hoaxes is obvious.

Deepfakes, as one type of generated video is called online, are spreading. They're named after the technique used to make them, a combination of "deep learning" and "fake." Deep learning is a category of machine learning and, like many other machine learning techniques, involves giving an algorithm a lot of pieces of data to "learn" from then asking it to generate some outcome—in the case of Deepfakes, the outcome being video (audio is not spoofed by the same technique). The results can be quite convincing already, and the technology and the technique are still improving.

In typical Internet fashion, Deepfake software was quickly adopted to swap out the porn stars in pornographic videos for other people. All it takes is a lot of pictures of the subject (the more the better) and someone familiar with the technique of creating the fakes. Thanks to Deepfakes, anyone and everyone can become a porn star—likely without wanting to be. Residents of Deepfakes discussion sites request videos of people including coworkers, classmates, and friends. The going rate, based on a 2018 article by *The Washington Post*, was just $20.[6]

Sites found themselves combating the new form of non-consensual porn. PornHub banned pornographic Deepfake videos from its service in early 2018, and moderators of the Deepfakes Reddit community tried to stop the slew of fake porn by tightening their rules.[7] Unsurprisingly, the efforts weren't particularly successful. PornHub didn't appear to be having success enforcing its ban and Reddit eventually removed its Deepfakes community for violating the site's policy against "involuntary pornography".[8]

Deepfake porn is more than a not-so-innocent pastime for some communities—it has also become a weapon for others to slut-shame and discredit rivals. It's something none of us are immune to because of the easy availability of pictures of us across the Internet—but some of us are more likely to be targeted than others. In May 2018, Rana Ayyub, a journalist in India, was digitally attacked for her work by individuals spreading a pornographic Deepfake video of her.

> The slut-shaming and hatred felt like being punished by a mob for my work as a journalist, an attempt to silence me. It was aimed at humiliating me, breaking me by trying to define me as a 'promiscuous,' 'immoral' woman.[9]

As effective as predatory Deepfakes porn is, there are limitations. Porn is relatively easy because it doesn't require sound. But, if we wanted to create a different hoax—like a political figure giving a speech—Deepfakes are only half the work. There's more to creating a hoax than just fake video, as effective as it can be in discrediting someone by putting them somewhere they weren't. For a full fabrication, we also need to make audio. And, that's coming soon.

LyreBird, a company behind sound editing technology, published a completely fabricated speech in 2018 given by Obama's voice. LyreBird hopes to use the technology that created the fake to help people who have lost the use of their voice. Adobe is developing similar software it calls VoCo, which the company describes as "Photoshop for audio."[10] Adobe says it intends to have safeguards to prevent misuse.

Technology for creating fake audio and video will make it harder to catch hoaxes and it could take fake news to catastrophic levels because we haven't learned to be suspicious of audio or video yet. Hany Farid, professor of computer science at the University of California, Berkeley, told *PBS* "I don't think it's an overstatement to say that it is a potential threat to democracy".[11]

As much as the technologies are being popularized by porn, Farid's concerns seem to be slowly coming true. In May 2018, Belgian political party sp.a circulated a video of Donald Trump addressing the people of Belgium about climate change.[12] The video was in english with Dutch subtitles for Belgian viewers, except for the last sentence which was left untranslated. In it, Trump told Belgium to withdraw from the Paris Agreement.

> As you know, I had the balls to withdraw from the Paris Climate Agreement, and so should you. Because what you guys are doing right now in Belgium is actually worse. You agreed, but you are not taking any measures, only bla bla bla bing bang boom. You even pollute more than before the agreement. Shame! Total shame! At least I am a fair person. People love me because I am a fair person. I'm the fairest person on Earth. So Belgium, don't be a hypocrite: withdraw from the Climate Agreement.

> [uncaptioned] We all know that climate change is fake, just like this video.[13]

The video and its audio, as its last line says, was fake. It was created using Adobe After Effects,[14] a video editing software that's widely used by studios. While After

Effects is a different software from that used to make Deepfakes, it illustrates how convincing fakes can be. Sp.a explained the video was intended to spark a discussion about climate change and to direct viewers to a petition pushing the Belgian government to take more drastic action. While the fake was imperfect—movements and splicing in the video were not quite right—it was convincing enough that people still fell for it. It shows that even an imperfect fake can be convincing enough to trick people.

> We have commissioned a professional studio to create this video, and we have checked with them that this is legally sound.[15]

There are technology-focused efforts in progress to protect us from these types of hoaxes. Farid has spent twenty years building forensic technology to uncover digital fakes and is careful to keep the details of his efforts quiet. "Once I spill on the research, all it takes is one asshole to add it to their system" he said to *The Guardian*.[16] In June 2018, University at Albany, SUNY, published a paper about a way to spot fakes, which creators will likely adapt to beat. Facebook has also created machine learning models to try to catch fakes posted by its users.

The fakes are getting better faster, however, and the problem is not just technological. Social media mob mentality means images don't need to be altered, they just need to surface with claims that they're relevant to current events. In several terrorist attacks, images circulated online that were claimed to be related to the attack, but were fake or completely unrelated to the attack they were supposedly from. In one case, the same manipulated image of an alleged perpetrator was circulated for two different, unrelated attacks, and even made it onto the front page of a Spanish newspaper that fell for the hoax.[17] Reddit's community has launched multiple vigilante investigations into attacks, and turned up the wrong suspect every time.

It isn't only the conspiracy-theorizing fringes of the Internet that get targeted. The bot-elevated #WalkAway campaign posted photos of Democrats who had allegedly walked away from the party, but many of the photos were traced back to stock image sites they were purchased from (though the campaign founder disavowed those tweets in a tweet of his own).[18] In 2017, an image of president Trump rescuing cats in Texas in the aftermath of Hurricane Harvey was shared over 18,000 times. The image was fake—it was an edited photo taken in 2008 in the state of Iowa and did not originally include Mr. Trump.[19]

The Internet hasn't learned from its mistakes though. Social media mob mentality and hoaxes still work and sometimes become the basis for conspiracy theories. It should come as no surprise that social media communities for well-known conspiracy theories exist, such as the flat earth society or those who think the moon landings were faked. Sometimes, the conspiracy theories spill into the real world and directly jeopardize our safety.

In 2017, a North Carolina man went on a hunt to prove an online conspiracy theory called "Pizzagate" which claimed a D.C. area pizzeria was being used to hold child sex slaves. The belief was based on his interpretation of a false story circulating on social media that connected Hillary Clinton's campaign adviser to the pizzeria, according to coded messages in leaked emails. Intending to rescue the children, he travelled to the Washington, D.C. restaurant at the middle of the conspiracy theory. During his rescue attempt the man fired three shots in the restaurant. Nobody was hurt, and he was sentenced to 48 months in jail.[20]

Another conspiracy, known as "QAnon," began to surface in the real world at Trump rallies in 2018. The conspiracy theory centers around an unknown individual known as "Q" who began posting enigmatic messages to various online forums after a comment from Mr. Trump about "the calm before the storm." Believers of the conspiracy theory think Q is a high ranking government official and have built interpretations around postings from Q that fill in the blanks and make sense of the enigmatic messages. Allegedly, according to Q, President Trump will expose and arrest members of the deep state. The theories as to the identity of Q ranged from Mr. Trump himself, to John F. Kennedy Jr., to Michael Flynn, to White House aid Dan Scavino.[21] In late 2018, a major QAnon account was traced to a failed Green Party congressional candidate from Arizona, and that account was later deleted. However, QAnon lives on.

Part of the reason these hoaxes spread so easily has more to do with social media habits than it does intelligence or media literacy. Social media magnifies the believability of false content. A 2016 study found that 59% of links shared on social media were never actually clicked and six in ten people were willing to share a link without reading the article it linked to.[22] The actual source of the post was apparently unimportant too, as researchers found most clicks on news stories on Twitter were generated from shares by regular users instead of the original news outlet. Those shares were often for much older stories than generally assumed.[23] Arnaud Legout, study co-author, explained further in a statement.

> People are more willing to share an article than read it. This is typical of modern information consumption. People form an opinion based on a summary, or a summary of summaries, without making the effort to go deeper.[24]

Interest targeting and "related content" make the problem worse by playing to confirmation bias and conferring legitimacy. Interest targeting has a tendency to hide some controversial content from us and show us the same things repeatedly, fooling our brains into thinking it must be accurate. The more we see a piece of information, true or not, the more likely we are to believe it. If our friends share it too we're more likely to trust it because we trust our friends.[25] This is a fact of how human psychology works and it's powerful. Confirmation bias can even make us doubt our senses if other people contradict them enough.[26]

We can see the effects of confirmation bias in an accelerated way by looking at what happens to content moderators. Not only are they exposed to the worst the Internet has to offer, but they're repeatedly exposed to fringe ideas and conspiracy theories. Eventually, based on a look at the industry from *The Verge*, they start to believe them—and something similar might be happening to us.

> The moderators told me it's a place where the conspiracy videos and memes that they see each day gradually lead them to embrace fringe views. One auditor walks the floor promoting the idea that the Earth is flat. A former employee told me he has begun to question certain aspects of the Holocaust. Another former employee, who told me he has mapped every escape route out of his house and sleeps with a gun at his side, said: "I no longer believe 9/11 was a terrorist attack."[27]

We're too ready to trust what we see on the Internet, especially if it's repetitive, reinforces our ideas, or is backed by the social media mob. We're not at the point where we're good at protecting ourselves from edited photos yet, and we're falling behind. But, we need to be careful not to swing too far in the other direction because we still need to be able to trust what's accurate, and to do so without political motivations.

The tools for creating fakes are getting better, but some of the more colorful concerns around them may be overblown. Photoshop, after all, didn't bring an apocalypse of fakes to the Internet. The problem is, our Internet is more social and more tailored now, and we're less likely to question what shows up in our feeds when it comes from our friends, or if we see it repeatedly. There will always be fakes, and they will always be improving—just as there will always be new conspiracy theories and viral disinformation campaigns for them to support. Whether the problem is ours to deal with or technology's, it's there and it's growing.

11 · THE BAITED

> I scroll around, but when I look at the
> internet, I feel the same as when I'm walking
> through Coney Island. It's like carnival
> barkers, and they all sit out there and go,
> "Come on in here and see a three-legged
> man!" So you walk in and it's a guy with a
> crutch—Former *Daily Show* host Jon Stewart[1]

If a site can't get our attention—or convince us to disable our ad blockers—it can't sell ad space. We're already browsing feeds that tailor things to our interests, with habit-forming features to keep us there. That poses a problem for other sites, which want to borrow our attention and capture us the same way— and with the same goal of showing us ads. To do that, sites need to make their content stand out from everything else in the news feed, based mainly on headlines. Unfortunately for us, they discovered that emotionally charged and often misleading headlines that play to our curiosity work best.[2] Thus, carnival barker style clickbait headlines were born.

The Oxford Dictionary defines clickbait as "content whose main purpose is to attract attention and encourage visitors to click on a link to a particular web page."[3] For some, the definition has blurred to include things they just disagree with. Even with the help of the dictionary definition, it's hard to describe exactly what a clickbait title is other than that once we're familiar with the Internet, we'll generally know one when we see one. Clickbait titles usually try to provide just enough information to make us curious but not enough to satisfy our curiosity so we'll be driven to click on the link.

The clickbait problem compounds on social media because being widely shared is also good for an article. Headlines intended to circulate widely through the social ecosystem are similar to clickbait but follow a slightly different format to make them more "shareable." Sharebait, as it's called, is a strategy used by sites that care more about social shares than clicks. It's used occasionally by legitimate news sites to circulate their brands, but has also propped up fake news sites that otherwise might never see enough traction to survive.

Sharebait works well because we trust posts from our social media friends—though we should be cautious about doing it blindly. Six in ten people will share headlines on Facebook without having ever opened the article.[4] What we see from friends factors into our decisions about what news we consume online. This has a wide-reaching effect because social shares, according to the same study, are important in deciding what news circulates and what news vanishes.

That's dangerous because social media isn't designed to be informative. Instead, it's designed to keep us coming back so it can sell more ads. The more habit-forming a social media site can be, such as by getting itself seen as a cure for boredom or by fuelling our fear of missing out, the better it is for business. Nir Eyal, author of *Hooked: How to Build Habit-Forming Products*, described the addictive nature of social media:

> I can alleviate my boredom, I can scratch that itch, just by scrolling through my newsfeed.
>
> What photos do people post? What are the comments going to say? How many likes do people get? It's a slot machine with lots of variability of what I might find.[5]

Although both trustworthy and questionable media outlets use clickbait, the content or veracity of the article across the link doesn't always matter. Only four in ten Americans reported they read articles beyond the headlines in a 2014 study.[6] If that study holds true, more than half of Americans may be accepting sensationalist clickbait headlines as fact. Because bait-style headlines are effective—even when we recognize them for what they are—we click on them and therefore train algorithms to show us more similar content.

Plenty of clickbait and sharebait articles are generally harmless time wasters. "What State Do You Actually Belong In?" and "Which Decade Do You Actually Belong In?" were two articles posted by *BuzzFeed* in 2014, prior to *BuzzFeed* telling us later that year that it didn't do clickbait.[7] There was little of substance in either, but they were good for quick entertainment.

Some bait headlines lead to worthwhile and accurate content. News outlets have adopted the same strategy because it's so effective. This is not, as some might like to believe, isolated to any particular ideological leaning. News websites across the ideological spectrum have used the number of clicks on an article as a factor in how much their writers got paid, as a metric for measuring how well their articles did, and for management decisions like promotions.[8] Inevitably, that created an incentive for writers to get as many clicks as possible—often with clickbait headlines—even if they might have preferred to write higher quality headlines. Fortunately, news sites have found other ways to measure success since 2014—but clickbait still grew in prevalence between 2014 and 2016.[9]

Other bait headlines though, are downright misleading, false, or harmful—and we sometimes fall for them even if we're told that they're false or satire. *America's Last Line of Defense*, a satirical Facebook page run by Christopher Blair in Maine, features the disclaimer "nothing on this page is real." The page is among the most popular Facebook destinations among Trump-supporting conservatives over the age of 55, most of whom do not recognize the page as satire.[10] Its total audience, as of late 2018, was over six million people. "No matter how racist, how bigoted, how offensive, how obviously fake we get, people keep coming back," Blair told *The New York Times*.[11] *America's Last Line of Defense* has posted made-up stories about California instituting sharia law, former president Bill Clinton becoming a serial killer, and undocumented immigrants defacing Mount Rushmore, often accompanied by the tagline "Share if you're outraged!"[12]

Blair's Facebook page is satire and marked as such, but its headlines resemble another problem: Yellow journalism. Yellow journalism poses as real journalism, but offers little to no legitimate news—often with headlines like Blair's. In the case of one yellow journalism site, LibertyWritersNews.com, the writers behind the site are purely focused on the profitability of bait headlines and don't believe in the content they write.[13] Headlines from the site include "THE TRUTH IS OUT! The Media Doesn't Want You To See What Hillary Did After Losing..." and are met with responses like "YOU ARE THE ONLY ONE I TRUST TO REPORT THE TRUTH" from regular readers.[14] The site's authors, Paris Wade and Ben Goldman, told the *Washington Post* they make so much money they felt uncomfortable talking about it.[15] Wade also told the *Washington Post* he wondered how it would feel to write an article he believed in.[16]

Clickbait and sharebait, whatever their sources, aren't small-scale problems, and may have effects on the political landscape. In the last three months of the 2016 presidential election, sharing of fake news on Facebook with bait-style headlines—much of which was pro-Trump or anti-Clinton—took the network by storm and overtook shares of factual news by about 1.4 million shares.[17] Facebook said shares don't indicate overall engagement with the articles, but the activity highlights how effective clickbait and sharebait techniques are at spreading headlines. Content that's interesting enough to share may not be content that's worthwhile while news that is worthwhile may not always be interesting enough to share.

Some social sites, including Facebook, have tried to offset misleading headlines by offering links to additional content their algorithms thought may be related to something we clicked on. On Facebook, these links appeared under a news feed post as "related content." Facebook intended the feature to provide additional perspectives on headlines, and has operated it in various forms (limited to certain countries) since 2014.[18] The algorithms didn't know if the original post was true, and could unintentionally imply legitimacy if they associated trusted sources with it.

Despite the best efforts of sites like Facebook, we're stuck grappling with dubious content for the foreseeable future. Yellow journalism, clickbait, targeted ads, and misplaced trust are likely to make fake news far worse before it gets better. Unfortunately, the ad revenue says the problem will grow unless we give better incentives for quality headlines and factual content. Our ability to know the truth of what's happening in the world is at risk—especially when we pair clickbait with misinformation campaigns and fabricated evidence. Until we change the incentives, the bait is probably here to stay. All we can do about it is read the article across the link and be skeptical of news sites that publish carnival-barker style headlines "that you wouldn't believe!"

12 · THE ADDICTS

> Once people come in, then the network effect
> kicks in and there's an overload of content.
> People click around. There's always another
> hashtag to click on. Then it takes on its own
> life, like an organism, and people can become
> obsessive—Greg Hochmuth[1]

"Facebook Addiction" has been a topic of numerous research papers and online articles about how to treat the condition. Greg Hochmuth, one of Instagram's first software engineers, described it in terms of the network effect. *CNN*'s senior medical correspondent published a piece about it in 2009.[2] Cornell Information Science labeled the inability to permanently leave social media "social media reversion" and discussed how hard it was for people to quit.

Even if a site is good at getting our attention, it also needs to hold onto it to maximize the value of its ad space. Using targeting similar to that used for ads, sites can tailor what they show—such as posts or news articles—to keep us engaged for as long as possible. The effect builds on itself. By keeping us longer, the site can also collect more behavioral information and better tailor its ads and content—and in some cases, its behavior towards us.

The problem is, content only goes so far. There are only so many news articles on or posts about other people's days we can read before we eventually want to move on to something new. Sites needed to find other ways to keep us occupied and coming back. In some cases, they landed on things that exploit our psychology in ways that make them hard for us to resist. A site may be willing to show us almost anything or give us any feature to keep us there, accuracy be damned—and if it's user-submitted content, the site itself isn't legally at fault for having created it.

The drive for a habit-forming social site isn't necessarily intentional—much of it is probably driven by comparing features to see what attracts the most visits. Addictive features might be somewhat accidental—but they are good at driving repeat visits. It's a result of a Silicon Valley culture shift from a desire to improve the world to trying to grow a site at almost all costs to turn a profit. Ellen Pao, former CEO of Reddit, discussed the shift with *NYMag* and went on to say that Reddit was no exception.

> It all goes back to Facebook. It was a success so quickly, and was so admired, that it changed the

culture. It went from 'I'm going to improve people's lives' to 'I'm going to build this product that everybody uses so I can make a lot of money.'[3]

The change has created an industry of "growth hackers" which specialize in using addictive techniques to grow sites. Companies consult with growth hackers with the hope of replicating Facebook's success. In April 2017, designers, developers, and entrepreneurs convened to take a $1,700 course organized by Nir Eyal about building habit-forming features into their products. Eyal, author of *Hooked: How to Build Habit-Forming Products,* has been helping Silicon Valley build addictive products for years. Other companies turn to services like GrowthHackers, which in 2018 listed Mozilla, Airbnb, and Spotify as some of its showcased clients,[4] and Dopamine Labs, a more controversial startup that makes its business clear from its name.

Dopamine Labs capitalizes on habit-forming features by using AI to tailor irregular rewards to individual users to maximize their effectiveness.[5] The company had ten clients as of early 2018, all of which had seen success from integrating the service into products. Results ranged from a 167% improvement in how often people sent each other encouraging messages in an anti-cyberbullying app, to an 11% improvement in food tracking in a dieting app. The types of rewards Dopamine Labs helps develop are tailored to the app: a running app, for example, might provide a virtual high five or confetti shower after a run—but only when the system decides the extra encouragement would be most effective.[6]

Even without the help of companies like GrowthHackers and Dopamine Labs, the services we use have stumbled on habit-forming features—so much so that many of the convenience features we expect are habit-forming. "Infinite scrolling" keeps loading more content as we scroll, so we never hit the bottom of a page and feel there's more to see. Notifications of all kinds keep us updated about what's going on even if we're not actually looking at the site, to fuel our fear of missing out. Auto-play makes it take more effort to stop watching than it does to just sit back and enjoy the next video or ten. They're features that we've come to expect from the apps and services we use. While they are convenient, they make it easier to stay connected than to walk away—and if we try to walk away, they draw us back in by reminding us that there might be something new to see.

And, there is usually something new to see. Ever-improving interest targeting picks the things we're most interested in so that we will keep scrolling for more. New content from our online friends, celebrities, and news that we're likely to agree with keeps our feeds fresh with things to "like" so we can perpetuate the cycle of dopamine. And of course, a fear of missing out on whatever the latest is in our social drama.

Sometimes, even features that seem like basic

functionality on the web are also contributors to addictive effects—including ones that we don't even think about such as "Pull-to-refresh." We expect pull-to-refresh in our connected apps because it feels like it's always been there and because it's almost everywhere. Yet, it can be an addictive feature. Some feel that pull-to-refresh is like pulling a level on a slot machine, complete with variable rewards.

Pull-to-refresh wasn't originally intended to be addictive. Loren Brichter, its inventor, couldn't find a place to put a refresh button in his startup's app in 2009, so he found a different way to add the feature. Though he didn't consider the way pull-to-refresh resembled a slot machine when he invented it, Brichter agreed with the sentiment of the comparison. He told *The Guardian* that he regretted the downsides to the overall addictive nature of our everyday technologies he inadvertently contributed to.

> Smartphones are useful tools. But they're addictive. Pull-to-refresh is addictive. Twitter is addictive. These are not good things. When I was working on them, it was not something I was mature enough to think about. I'm not saying I'm mature now, but I'm a little bit more mature, and I regret the downsides.[7]

Brichter pointed out to *The Guardian* that although pull-to-refresh is still a standard app feature, it is no longer needed. Better technology allows apps to pull content from their backing services automatically, similar to how they can show notifications without being asked. In modern apps, the feature appears to be geared less towards necessary functionality and more towards fulfilling user expectations. In that context, Brichter preferred to compare the feature to the close door button on certain elevators that does nothing.[8]

Whether addictive effects are by design or by accident, research shows that they can be real. Citing data from 99DaysOfFreedom.com, a site that tried to encourage leaving Facebook for 99 days, Cornell Information Science found that participants wanted to quit and believed they could quit, but many weren't able to make it more than a few days. People who thought Facebook was an addictive service were more likely to have a problem staying away, while those with other motivations or distractions—such as using other social media or having privacy concerns centered around Facebook—were more likely to succeed in staying away.[9] Articles like *CNN*'s about the addictive nature of social media help shape those perceptions and magnify addictive effects.

Concern about the habit-forming features of our social media has expanded to Silicon Valley's own residents, including Brichter. A group of former Silicon Valley employees—mainly engineers—is working to counter the utopian narrative of social media companies. Among other things, the group believes the modern social media ecosystem has a negative effect on the political system. Its members suggest that social media, if left unchecked, could upend democracy if it hasn't already. They're serious enough that they don't use the popular products of Silicon Valley, and they send their kids to schools that ban devices like laptops and iPads.

Justin Rosenstein, one concerned Silicon Valley engineer and the engineer behind the Facebook "like" button, configured his laptop to block Reddit, removed himself from Snapchat, and limited his use of Facebook. He was concerned that we're running out of time to talk about social media and its effects.

> One reason I think it is particularly important
> for us to talk about this now is that we may be
> the last generation that can remember life
> before.[10]

Chamath Palihapitiya, a former Facebook executive, and Sean Parker, a former Facebook president, held similar views.[11] They, too, worried what Facebook and other addicting sites might be doing to society and to democracies. The view, at least for Palihapitiya, didn't appear to borne out of malice towards a former employer. Palihapitiya said in an interview at Stanford that Facebook was still a company he loved, but was very blunt about how he saw the service's place in the world.

> The short-term, dopamine-driven feedback
> loops that we have created are destroying how
> society works: no civil discourse, no
> cooperation, misinformation, mistruth. It is

> eroding the core foundations of how people
> behave by and between each other. I don't have
> a good solution. My solution is I just don't use
> these tools anymore.[12]

Not everyone shared the same feelings about habit-forming features. Eyal defended the strategies he taught —but surprised his 2017 audience by including ways to resist them. "Just as we shouldn't blame the baker for making such delicious treats, we can't blame tech makers for making their products so good we want to use them."[13] Engineers Justin Santamaria and Chris Marcellino, listed on Apple's patent for notification features including the "unread" count on app icons, also didn't fault themselves. Santamaria told *The Guardian* that the technology wasn't "inherently good or bad" and suggested that instead there was a bigger question about whether it's okay to disconnect in certain circumstances.[14] Marcellino agreed.

> Honestly, at no point was I sitting there
> thinking: let's hook people. It was all about the
> positives: these apps connect people, they have
> all these uses – ESPN telling you the game has
> ended, or WhatsApp giving you a message for
> free from your family member in Iran who
> doesn't have a message plan.[15]

Marcellino didn't deny that those features could be addictive, however. As of 2017 he was in the midst of a career change, and in the late stages of schooling to become a neurosurgeon. He told *The Guardian* that medical training gave him enough information to know that technologies like the ones he worked on could be addicting. "These are the same circuits that make people seek out food, comfort, heat, sex."[16]

Our brains weren't built for the Internet we created, and the problem isn't our willpower. Tristan Harris, a design ethicist and product philosopher at Google suggested we're fighting a losing battle against habit-forming features.

> The 'I don't have enough willpower'
> conversation misses the fact that there are 1,000
> people on the other side of the screen whose job
> is to break down the self-regulation that you
> have.[17]

Unfortunately, the incentives for companies are so rooted in growth that even tech executives who might want to design their products in a better way aren't able to. While companies probably didn't get founded with the express intent of becoming addictive and didn't intend to become addictive—something Harris and Marcellino suggested—many now are. Until we create incentives for services to help us build healthy relationships with our technology, habit-forming products are unlikely to change their ways—they have shareholders to answer to and employees to pay. We're getting trapped in ways we never envisioned, by services that care increasingly about profiting off of our presence and less about connecting us.

13 · THE INHABITANTS

> What the Internet hucksters won't tell you is
> that the Internet is one big ocean of unedited
> data, without any pretense of completeness.
> Lacking editors, reviewers or critics, the
> Internet has become a wasteland of unfiltered
> data. You don't know what to ignore and
> what's worth reading—Clifford Stoll[1]

While he missed the mark on some things which were beyond the bounds of technology at the time, astronomer and computer expert Clifford Stoll's concerns about the Internet's social effects and trustworthiness were well grounded. More than two decades later the Internet is still fighting similar problems: increasingly convincing fake news runs rampant, too much "filtering" as Stoll might describe it gives us all our own social feeds that are increasingly divorced from reality, and we've learned how to disrupt conversations with armies of bots, paid influencers, and volunteer thought police. And, it's getting easier to make all those things happen.

Need a Twitter bot? There are step-by-step guides for building one, with code you can copy and paste.[2]

Need a Twitter army? Run your bot with a list of accounts.

Need a social media personality? Steal photos and make up stories. Nobody would know the difference.[3]

Need to discredit someone by putting them into a video they didn't appear in? $20 and a lot of photos of them is all you need if you know where to ask for Deepfake porn.[4]

If you don't code, you can copy-paste from a quick web search, or use a bot creation software. And there are valid reasons to do some of these things—making sure a website can handle that many hits or retweeting breaking news. Just as easily though, those tools can be used unethically, illegally, and immorally—and they are. Accusations of foreign interference in elections are no longer surprising headlines, sites are fighting Deepfake porn, and social sites have been taking down millions of fake accounts.

Although the problems are familiar, the Internet Stoll described was very different from the one we use today. Ordering a pizza online was a novelty, and only possible if you lived in Santa Cruz.[5] What exactly the web would become was unknown, but it was changing how people communicated in ways we would recognize. Social media's early beginnings were in place as Usenet, BBS, and various other services. The still-familiar companies weren't around yet. AOL wasn't ready to make its mark until 1997, MySpace appeared in 2003, and Facebook in 2004.[6]

In some ways, our web is better now. We created places that are safer and more accessible, with rules and moderation. These are the well-cultivated walled gardens of major social media sites, app stores, and ecosystems of services. Their walls keep many dangerous things like malware out. Tools for reporting and hiding harassment, abuse, or anything we just happen to disagree with are never more than a few clicks away. Creators have better tools for protecting their rights and for preventing the theft of their intellectual property, as well as more options for publishing and marketing it.

And, for all its faults, the web is still a place where free speech reigns—for as long as the services we use and the infrastructure providers that power them respect it. It's a core value of the Internet, and an important one. The American Civil Liberties Union (ACLU) agrees, and says that strong free speech protections for all are more important than censoring bigotry, and defends even the most hateful of legal speech from censorship.[7] The promise of free speech gives us—in some countries— the ability to share our thoughts on the Internet, to publish books like this one, and to connect with people around the world.

But, although something can be published, that doesn't mean it's worth our while. The promise of free speech gave everyone from the best and brightest to the person yelling about conspiracy theories in an empty corner of a public park the same platform. It's noisy—our feeds are full of things that aren't true, aren't relevant, or aren't important to us and it takes us effort to sort through the flood of content. It's a problem Stoll described from an earlier Internet.

> Consider today's online world. The Usenet, a worldwide bulletin board, allows anyone to post messages across the nation. Your word gets out, leapfrogging editors and publishers. Every voice can be heard cheaply and instantly. The result? Every voice is heard. The cacophany [sic] more closely resembles citizens band radio, complete with handles, harrasment [sic], and anonymous threats.[8]

In the hope of solving those problems, we turned to companies. We wanted our feeds to give us localized and tailored information—to cut out some noise and to save us time searching. Services started tracking our behavior and gave us what we asked for in return for our anonymity. We asked for moderation in our social communities, app stores, and messaging to keep malware and harassment out. Services gave us "report abuse" buttons and AI to keep our feeds clean. The more we asked for, the more companies were willing to give us if it kept us within their walls—even if it didn't solve the problems we faced. Many of the features that hurt our ability to connect with the world around us are ones we asked for, learned to love, and grew accustomed to.

As part of the evolution we pushed for, the digital landscape changed. Open standards like RSS and oEmbed saw their peak—complete with excited announcements from social sites about how far across the web we could take our content—then their fall as services discovered that it was more profitable to close us in. Online advertising grew from simple ads to a hundred billion dollar industry[9] that invades our online experience with interruptions and extremely specific targeting. We don't know why our feeds show us what we see, why they don't show us what we don't see, or what they know about us.

Although what we see is targeted, the targeting hasn't helped. Their algorithms are designed to keep our attention as much as possible, and have trouble dealing with false or abusive content. Our feeds are still noisy, but what they show us is better targeted and we're more likely to believe it. Although the curation itself might be apolitical, it's not neutral, as psychology professor Colleen Seifert at the University of Michigan, told *The New York Times*.

> People have a benevolent view of Facebook, for instance, as a curator, but in fact it does have a motive of its own. What it's actually doing is

keeping your eyes on the site. It's curating news
and information that will keep you watching.[10]

Seifert's views are mirrored by those of Yuval Noah
Harari, an Israeli historian and writer of two bestsellers.
He suggested that profits are a reason for the spread of
fake news and why we accept it. In an interview with
The Guardian he discussed the modern Internet and the
direction companies have moved.

At present there is an incentive in order to get
your attention – and then sell it to advertisers
and politicians and so forth – to create more and
more sensational stories, irrespective of truth or
relevance. Some of the fake news comes from
manipulation by Russian hackers but much of it
is simply because of the wrong incentive
structure. There is no penalty for creating a
sensational story that is not true. We're willing
to pay for high quality food and clothes and
cars, so why not high quality information?[11]

Along the way, the companies grew too. Their services
are now so large that they're changing the very nature
of the Internet. Facebook finds itself used by over 68%
of adults in the U.S.[12] Problems with single
infrastructure providers can affect more than hundreds
of thousands to millions of websites. At the time of its
major 2017 outage, Amazon Web Services (Amazon S3,
to be exact) was used by about 148,000 websites,
including 0.8% of the top one million websites on the
Internet.[13] Cloudflare claimed to be handling 10% of

Internet requests the same year.[14]

At the scale they operate at, we should worry about their stewardship of the Internet. We should worry about bias in the features they gave us, especially in terms of moderation and content suggestions. Human moderators make mistakes—and even when they don't, they're following corporate policies which might not have our best interests in mind.[15] Facebook shut down its trending headlines feature after problems with bias and fake news.[16] Algorithms have been known to act on the unconscious biases of the people who built them and in some cases are poorly understood even by the engineers who worked on them. "Even the creators don't always understand why it recommends one video instead of another," Guillaume Chaslot, a former YouTube engineer, told *Wired* of YouTube's suggestion algorithm.[17] In some cases, the algorithms surface conspiracy theories and fake news as easily as they do factual content.

We're ill-equipped to deal with the Internet that they created for us. Apps and websites exploit our biology to keep us coming back for the pseudo-pleasure they provide while pushing us further apart in the real world.[18] Digital communities are increasingly splitting along political lines and in some cases are excluding people from the community they physically live in. Some evidence even shows that we've reached a point where trying to burst our filter bubbles actually makes us more politically extreme. According to the study, "well-intentioned attempts to introduce people to opposing political views on social media might not only be ineffective, but counter-productive."[19]

But, the services and secret algorithms that we're quick to blame when something bad happens aren't the only problem. The other problem is the online culture we've developed. For many, seeing something on the Internet gives it credibility, because our carefully curated social circle obviously wouldn't lie to us. But, lie it does. The majority of things shared on social media are never read past their headlines, so we don't know if what our friends share is real—but we'll probably re-share it anyway.[20]

We didn't consider the fakes, the bot armies, and the paid influencers that steer our conversation. And, we didn't ask for the transparency from our feeds that would empower us to make decisions about the content we trust and consume. It makes it easy for some forms of modern propaganda to invade our feeds and manipulate our opinions. There isn't any need to silence or threaten people anymore because propagandists can manipulate us other ways. *Wired* writer Zeynep Tufekci described what modern censorship looks like online—a big difference from the days of shutting down newspapers.

> The most effective forms of censorship today involve meddling with trust and attention, not muzzling speech.[21]

We're seeing the effects of the Internet we created. Evidence of war crimes is vanishing behind the moderation systems of social media, making it harder for human rights groups to document atrocities and for courts to prosecute those behind the atrocities.[22] Search engines uncover propaganda, misinformation, and occasionally conspiracy theories or fake news sometimes as easily as they do real information.[23] Vigilante defenders of ideas are learning how to use the features of social media to make things they don't like disappear.[24] Bot armies have risen to defend attacks on other countries,[25] to slander politicians,[26] and to disrupt news and peaceful protests.[27] Foreign groups have organized protests and counter-protests in the same place at the same time to pit groups against each other.[28]

We're learning, but we still fall for things that we want to believe. We share photos thousands of times that we haven't verified, such as President Trump rescuing cats from Hurricane Harvey in Texas (the photos did not originally include Mr. Trump and were not taken in Texas).[29] Although we know hoax photos exist, fabricated audio and video are hardly on our radar—but they're here. Online communities are facing "involuntary pornography," as Reddit refers to it, people spliced convincingly into pornographic videos for the entertainment of some, and the discrediting of others.[30] Completely fabricated speeches from former president Barack Obama have been shared by companies working on better CGI and assistive technologies that they hope to make available in the near future.[31] Similar fakes have already made it into the hands of groups with political motives, with a video of Mr. Trump giving a speech he'd never given surfacing in 2018 from a Belgian political party.[32]

If we don't find solutions to these problems, they will get worse. The algorithms that curate our feeds are ill-equipped to protect us and are already failing to. Ever-improving technology means the protections we see today might soon be obsolete. Even where the algorithms succeed, they're often also hiding the realities of our world, while showing us propaganda and questionable information—and we don't know the reasons for their decisions.

The Washington Post's tagline says "democracy dies in darkness." Nobody yet knows what democracy does in cyberspace. But, they seem to be at odds. As we sink deeper into the trap of Deepfakes, profit-driven interest targeting, moderated communities, and influencer armies, some, including former Silicon Valley employees, are raising the alarm. It's up to us to hold the cloud accountable in order to build an Internet for everyone that empowers us to be informed citizens. What will our Internet, and from its influence, our real-world communities look like across this threshold?

ACKNOWLEDGEMENTS

No book is written in isolation, and *The Thought Trap* is no exception. I extend my gratitude to the various people who helped along the way by offering their support, encouragement, and understanding. Without their help to keep me going and to remind me that second-guessing myself was almost never useful, this book might not have been finished.

Special thanks needs to, once again, go to Seth for putting up with the musings, delayed housework, and general insanity of living with someone writing a book yet again. Hopefully, having done this before my process was less absurd—or you just noticed less. I don't remember having as many late dinners this time around.

Of course, thank you to the many authors and technologists who are cited throughout *The Thought Trap* for their research and work that this book is built on top of.

Last but not least, a thank-you needs to be extended to you, reader. I hope that you found your time with this book as worthwhile as I found my time producing it. Without your support, independent authors like myself would never see their work read.

ABOUT THE AUTHOR

Nate Levesque is a software engineer, independent author, and digital rights advocate. He writes about technology and digital rights, including his blog, his other book, *Please Upgrade for Access,* and has written for Opensource.com. Nate holds a degree in software engineering from the Rochester Institute of Technology, and builds networking products at his day job.

www.natelevesque.com

NOTES

1. Russell Brandom, "Facebook's Report Abuse Button Has Become a Tool of Global Oppression," September 2, 2014, https://www.theverge.com/2014/9/2/6083647/facebook-s-report-abuse-button-has-become-a-tool-of-global-oppression.

2. Brandom.

3. Brandom.

4. Michael Pizzi, "The Syrian Opposition Is Disappearing From Facebook," *The Atlantic*, February 4, 2014, https://www.theatlantic.com/international/archive/2014/02/the-syrian-opposition-is-disappearing-from-facebook/283562/

5. Brandom.

6. Avi Asher-Schapiro, "YouTube and Facebook Are Removing Evidence of Atrocities, Jeopardizing Cases Against War Criminals," *The Intercept* (blog), November 2, 2017, https://theintercept.com/2017/11/02/war-crimes-youtube-facebook-syria-rohingya/.

7. Asher-Schapiro

8. Asher-Schapiro

9. "More Information, Faster Removals, More People · an Update on What We're Doing to Enforce YouTube's Community Guidelines," *Official YouTube Blog* (blog), April 23, 2018, https://youtube.googleblog.com/2018/04/more-information-faster-removals-more.html.

147

10. Asher-Schapiro, "YouTube and Facebook Are Removing Evidence of Atrocities, Jeopardizing Cases Against War Criminals."

11. Asher-Schapiro

12. Joel Kaplan and Justin Osofsky, "Input From Community and Partners On Our Community Standards | Facebook Newsroom," *Facebook Newsroom* (blog), October 21, 2016, https://newsroom.fb.com/news/2016/10/input-from-community-and-partners-on-our-community-standards/.

13. Asher-Schapiro, "YouTube and Facebook Are Removing Evidence of Atrocities, Jeopardizing Cases Against War Criminals."

14. Asher-Schapiro.

15. Jessica Anderson et al., "Censorship In Context," November 16, 2016, https://onlinecensorship.org/news-and-analysis/onlinecensorship-org-launches-second-report-censorship-in-context-pdf.

16. Nga Pham, "Hanoi Admits Online Interference," January 12, 2013, sec. Asia, https://www.bbc.com/news/world-asia-20982985.

17. Mai Ngoc Chau, "Vietnam Deploys 10,000 Cyber Warriors to Fight 'Wrongful Views,'" December 26, 2017, https://www.bloomberg.com/news/articles/2017-12-27/vietnam-deploys-10-000-cyber-warriors-to-fight-wrongful-views.

18. Jessica Anderson et al., "Censorship In Context."

THE MODERATORS

1. Matthew Prince, "Why We Terminated Daily Stormer," *The Cloudflare Blog* (blog), August 16, 2017, https://blog.cloudflare.com/why-we-terminated-daily-stormer/.

2. Russell Brandom, "Charlottesville Is Reshaping the Fight against Online Hate," The Verge, August 15, 2017, https://www.theverge.com/2017/8/15/16151740/charlottesville-daily-stormer-ban-neo-nazi-facebook-censorship.

3. Timothy B. Lee, "Racist Daily Stormer moves to Russian domain after losing .com address [Updated]," Ars Technica, August 16, 2017, https://arstechnica.com/tech-policy/2017/08/shunned-by-godaddy-and-google-racist-daily-stormer-moves-to-russian-domain/.

4. Brandom, "Charlottesville Is Reshaping the Fight against Online Hate."

5. Matthew Prince, "Why We Terminated Daily Stormer."

6. Michael Edison Hayden, "Neo-Nazi Website Daily Stormer Is 'Designed to Target Children' as Young as 11, Editor Boasts," Newsweek, January 16, 2018, https://www.newsweek.com/website-daily-stormer-designed-target-children-editor-claims-782401.

7. Brandom, "Charlottesville Is Reshaping the Fight against Online Hate."

8. Brandom.

9. Catherine Buni and Soraya Chemaly, "The Secret Rules of the Internet," The Verge, April 13, 2016, https://www.theverge.com/2016/4/13/11387934/internet-moderator-history-youtube-facebook-reddit-censorship-free-speech.

10. Brandom, "Charlottesville Is Reshaping the Fight against Online Hate."

11. Gene Puskar, "Gunman Attacks Pittsburgh Synagogue, Killing 11 People," PBS NewsHour, October 27, 2018, https://www.pbs.org/newshour/nation/pittsburgh-synagogue-shooter-opened-fire-during-baby-naming-ceremony.

12. Brandon Wall, "Racist Reddit Group Embraces Alleged Charleston Shooting Manifesto," BuzzFeed News, June 20, 2015, https://www.buzzfeednews.com/article/brandonwall/racist-reddit-group-embraces-alleged-charleston-shooting-man.

13. Mike Wendling, "What Should Social Networks Do about Hate Speech?," June 29, 2015, sec. Trending, https://www.bbc.com/news/blogs-trending-33288367.

14. Casey Newton, "The Secret Lives of Facebook Moderators in America," The Verge, February 25, 2019, https://www.theverge.com/2019/2/25/18229714/cognizant-facebook-content-moderator-interviews-trauma-working-conditions-arizona.

15. Rad Campaign, Lincoln Park Strategies, and Craigconnects, "The Rise of Online Harassment," 2016, http://onlineharassmentdata.org/2018/.

16. Rad Campaign, Lincoln Park Strategies, and Craigconnects.

17. Mitch van Geel, Paul Vedder, and Jenny Tanilon, "Relationship Between Peer Victimization, Cyberbullying, and Suicide in Children and Adolescents: A Meta-Analysis," *JAMA Pediatrics* 168, no. 5 (May 1, 2014): 435, https://doi.org/10.1001/jamapediatrics.2013.4143.

18. Lucas Shaw, "YouTube Advertising Crackdown Puts Some Creators Out of Work," December 8, 2017, https://www.bloomberg.com/news/articles/2017-12-08/youtube-

advertising-crackdown-puts-some-creators-out-of-work.

19. Jeff D'Onofrio, "A Better, More Positive Tumblr," *Tumblr Staff* (blog), December 3, 2018, https://staff.tumblr.com/post/180758987165/a-better-more-positive-tumblr.

20. Cassidy Dawn Graves, "Tumblr Users Spent Years Reporting Child Porn. They Say the Site Ignored Them," MEL Magazine, December 12, 2018, https://melmagazine.com/en-us/story/tumblr-child-pornography-problem.

21. Jason Koebler and Matthew Gault, "A Quarter of Tumblr's Users Are There to Consume Porn, Data Scientists Estimate," *Motherboard* (blog), December 5, 2018, https://motherboard.vice.com/en_us/article/gy7w4b/data-scientists-estimate-a-quarter-of-tumblrs-users-are-there-to-consume-porn.

22. "Pornhub ARIA on Twitter: 'Tumblrs: Pornhub Welcomes You with Open Arms. Join Our Amazing Community of Millions Curators: Customize Your Personal Feed, Create Playlists, Generate Gifs and More Creators: Upload Videos, Photos, Gifs & Share Text Posts to a Massive Audience. Earn Revenue on Your Content.' / Twitter," Twitter, accessed July 28, 2019, https://twitter.com/pornhub/status/1069984706521747458.

23. Ankita Rao, "Social Media Companies Are Not Free Speech Platforms," *Motherboard* (blog), November 25, 2016, https://motherboard.vice.com/en_us/article/4xa5v9/social-media-companies-are-not-free-speech-platforms.

24. "Site Information - FAQ, Privacy Policy, Advertising And More | Pornhub," accessed June 28, 2019, https://www.pornhub.com/information#terms.

THE DIVIDERS

1. Eli Pariser, *The Filter Bubble: What the Internet Is Hiding From You* (Penguin Press, 2011).

2. Mostafa M. El-Bermawy, "Your Filter Bubble Is Destroying Democracy," *Wired*, November 18, 2016, https://www.wired.com/2016/11/filter-bubble-destroying-democracy/.

3. Aaron Smith, "The Internet's Role in Campaign 2008 | Pew Research Center," April 15, 2009, https://www.pewinternet.org/2009/04/15/the-internets-role-in-

campaign-2008/.

4. William Brady et al., "Emotion Shapes the Diffusion of Moralized Content in Social Networks," *Proceedings of the National Academy of Sciences* 114 (June 26, 2017): 201618923, https://doi.org/10.1073/pnas.1618923114.

5. Jon Martindale, "Fake News and Filter Bubbles – It's Our Job to Stop Them," Digital Trends, December 6, 2016, https://www.digitaltrends.com/social-media/fake-news-and-filter-bubbles/.

6. El-Bermawy, "Your Filter Bubble Is Destroying Democracy."

7. Jeffrey Gottfried and Elisa Shearer, "News Use Across Social Media Platforms 2016 | Pew Research Center," May 26, 2016, https://www.journalism.org/2016/05/26/news-use-across-social-media-platforms-2016/.

8. Martindale.

9. Will Oremus, "A Surprising New Study Suggests the Internet Isn't Tearing Us Apart After All," Slate Magazine, April 5, 2017, https://slate.com/technology/2017/04/filter-bubbles-revisited-the-internet-may-not-be-driving-political-polarization.html.

10. Oremus.

11. Kevin J. Delaney, "Filter Bubbles Are a Serious Problem with News, Says Bill Gates," Quartz, February 21, 2017, https://qz.com/913114/bill-gates-says-filter-bubbles-are-a-serious-problem-with-news/.

12. Lars Backstrom, "News Feed FYI: A Window Into News Feed," Facebook for Business, August 6, 2013, https://www.facebook.com/business/news/News-Feed-FYI-A-Window-Into-News-Feed.

13. Lars Backstrom, "News Feed FYI: A Window Into News Feed," Facebook for Business, August 6, 2013, https://www.facebook.com/business/news/News-Feed-FYI-A-Window-Into-News-Feed.

14. Josh Constine, "Facebook Launches Trending Topics On Web With Descriptions Of Why Each Is Popular," *TechCrunch* (blog), January 16, 2014, http://social.techcrunch.com/2014/01/16/facebook-trending/.

15. Michael Nunez, "Former Facebook Workers: We Routinely Suppressed Conservative News," Gizmodo, accessed June 6, 2018, https://gizmodo.com/former-facebook-workers-we-routinely-suppressed-conser-1775461006.

16. Nunez.

17. Vindu Goel and Ravi Somaiya.

18. Barbara Ortutay, "Facebook Kills 'trending' Topics, Tests Breaking News Label," AP NEWS, June 1, 2018, https://apnews.com/91af6216e641494eabda1b17463147d3.

19. Karen Hao, "Google Is Making It Easier for You to Only See What You Want To," Quartz, July 5, 2017, https://qz.com/1034058/googles-goog-updated-mobile-search-app-may-make-filter-bubbles-even-hard-to-escape/.

20. "About - Google News Initiative," Google News Initiative, accessed June 2, 2019, https://newsinitiative.withgoogle.com/about/.

21. "About the Facebook Journalism Project," Facebook Journalism Project, accessed June 2, 2019, https://facebookjournalismproject.com/about/.

22. Megan McQueen, "Fishing for Truth: Politics in the Era of Clickbait Journalism," *The Politic* (blog), February 10, 2017, http://thepolitic.org/fishing-for-truth-politics-in-the-era-of-clickbait-journalism/.

THE INTEGRATORS

1. Nicholas Carr, "The Cloud Giveth and the Cloud Taketh Away," *ROUGH TYPE* (blog), November 23, 2011, http://www.roughtype.com/?p=1553.

2. Nicholas Carr, "Tools, Platforms, and Google Reader," *ROUGH TYPE* (blog), March 14, 2013, http://www.roughtype.com/?p=3077.

3. Ryan Holmes, "From Inside Walled Gardens, Social Networks Are Suffocating The Internet As We Know It," Fast Company, August 9, 2013, https://www.fastcompany.com/3015418/from-inside-walled-gardens-social-networks-are-suffocating-the-internet-as-we-know-it.

4. Holmes.

5. Josh Catone, "The Rise of Twitter as a Platform for Serious Discourse," *ReadWrite* (blog), January 30, 2008, https://readwrite.com/2008/01/30/the_rise_of_twitter_as_a_platform_for_serious_discourse/.

6. Holmes, "From Inside Walled Gardens, Social Networks Are Suffocating The Internet As We Know It"

7. Catone, "The Rise of Twitter as a Platform for Serious Discourse"

8. Michael Arrington, "Facebook Launches Facebook Platform; They Are the Anti-MySpace," *TechCrunch* (blog), accessed January 29, 2019, http://social.techcrunch.com/2007/05/24/facebook-launches-facebook-platform-they-are-the-anti-myspace/.

9. Jeremy Keith, "Adactio: Journal—Battle for the Planet of the APIs," *Adactio* (blog), June 17, 2013, https://adactio.com/journal/6291.

10. Holmes, "From Inside Walled Gardens, Social Networks Are Suffocating The Internet As We Know It."

11. Michael Sippey, "Delivering a Consistent Twitter Experience," *Developer Blog* (blog), June 29, 2012, https://blog.twitter.com/developer/en_us/a/2012/delivering-consistent-twitter-experience.html.

12. Holmes, "From Inside Walled Gardens, Social Networks Are Suffocating The Internet As We Know It."

13. Will Critchlow, "What You Need to Know About Accelerated Mobile Pages (AMPs) - Whiteboard Friday," Moz, December 18, 2015, https://moz.com/blog/accelerated-mobile-pages-whiteboard-friday

14. Facebook, "Instant Articles," accessed July 3, 2019, https://instantarticles.fb.com

15. Dieter Bohn, "Google Takes a Tiny Step toward Fixing AMP's URL Problem," The Verge, April 16, 2019, https://www.theverge.com/2019/4/16/18402628/google-amp-url-problem-signed-exchange-original-chrome-cloudflare.

16. Anil Dash, "The Web We Lost," *Anil Dash* (blog), December 13, 2012, https://anildash.com/2012/12/13/the_web_we_lost/.

17. Mathew Ingram, "War Is Hell: Welcome to the Twitter Wars of 2011," February 18, 2011, https://gigaom.com/2011/02/18/war-is-hell-welcome-to-the-twitter-wars-of-2011/.

18. Mazin Sidahmed, "Dennis Cooper Fears Censorship as Google Erases Blog without Warning," *The Guardian*, July 14, 2016, sec. Books, https://www.theguardian.com/books/2016/jul/14/dennis-cooper-google-censorship-dc-blog.

19. Mazin Sidahmed, "Dennis Cooper's Blog Re-Launched after Google Censorship Criticisms," *The Guardian*, August 31, 2016, sec. Books, https://www.theguardian.com/books/2016/aug/31/dennis-cooper-dcs-blog-relaunched-google-censorship.

20. Sidahmed, "Dennis Cooper Fears Censorship as Google Erases Blog without Warning."

21. "Digital Pricing Page," Amazon Kindle Direct Publishing, accessed January 29, 2019, https://kdp.amazon.com/en_US/help/topic/G200644210.

22. Mathew Ingram, "Amazon, Lendle and the Danger of Using Open APIs," March 22, 2011, https://gigaom.com/2011/03/22/amazon-lendle-and-the-dangers-of-using-someone-elses-api/.

23. The iFlowReader Staff, "Free EBooks on the #1 Rated EBook Reader for IPhone, IPad, and IPod Touch," June 15, 2011, https://web.archive.org/web/20110615031108/http://www.iflowreader.com/Closing.aspx.

24. "A Letter about Google AMP," January 9, 2018, http://ampletter.org.

THE MERCHANTS

1. Richard Stallman, "Letter to the Boston Public Library — Free Software Foundation — Working Together for Free Software," January 30, 2006, https://www.fsf.org/campaigns/bpl.html.

2. Brad Stone, "Amazon Erases Orwell Books From Kindle Devices," *The New York Times*, July 17, 2009, sec. Technology, https://www.nytimes.com/2009/07/18/technology/companies/18amazon.html.

3. Stone.

4. Eileen Brown, "Why Amazon Is within Its Rights to Remove Access to Your Kindle Books," ZDNet, accessed March 25, 2018, https://www.zdnet.com/article/why-amazon-is-within-its-rights-to-remove-access-to-your-kindle-books/.

5. "Conditions of Use," Amazon.com, accessed February 16, 2019, https://www.amazon.com/gp/help/customer/display.html?nodeId=201909000.

6. Jason Koebler, "Why American Farmers Are Hacking Their Tractors With Ukrainian Firmware," March 21, 2017, https://www.vice.com/en_us/article/xykkkd/why-american-farmers-are-hacking-their-tractors-with-ukrainian-firmware.

7. "Books in Microsoft Store: FAQ," Microsoft Store Support, April 2, 2019, https://support.microsoft.com/en-us/help/4497396/books-in-microsoft-store-faq.

8. Karl Bode, "Microsoft Ebooks Will Stop Working Because It's Shutting Down a DRM Server," July 1, 2019,

https://www.vice.com/en_us/article/3k3wkk/microsoft-ebooks-will-stop-working-because-its-shutting-down-a-drm-server.

9. Erik Sherman, "Amazon Execs Can't Define Porn, but They Know It When They See It," January 10, 2011, https://www.cbsnews.com/news/amazon-execs-cant-define-porn-but-they-know-it-when-they-see-it/.

10. Esmeralda Greene, "WTF, Amazon?," *Esmeralda Greene's Blog* (blog), December 14, 2010, http://www.esmeraldagreene.com/EsmeraldaGreene/Blog/Entries/2010/12/14_WTF,_Amazon_2.html.

11. Erik Sherman, "Amazon Execs Can't Define Porn, but They Know It When They See It."

12. "Content Guidelines," Amazon.com, accessed July 3, 2018, https://www.amazon.com/gp/help/customer/display.html?nodeId=15015801.

13. Erik Sherman, "Amazon's Conflicting Censorship Stories Show Problems [UPDATED]," April 14, 2009, https://www.cbsnews.com/news/amazons-conflicting-censorship-stories-show-problems-updated/.

14. "February 2017 Big, Bad, Wide & International Report: Covering Amazon, Apple, B&N, and Kobo Ebook Sales in the US, UK, Canada, Australia, and New Zealand," Author Earnings, February 2017, http://authorearnings.com/report/february-2017/.

15. James Vincent, "99.6 Percent of New Smartphones Run Android or IOS," The Verge, February 16, 2017, https://www.theverge.com/2017/2/16/14634656/android-ios-market-share-blackberry-2016.

16. Devin Coldewey, "Alt-Social Network Gab Booted from Google Play Store for Hate Speech," *TechCrunch* (blog), August 7, 2017, http://social.techcrunch.com/2017/08/17/alt-social-network-gab-booted-from-google-play-store-for-hate-speech/.

17. Devin Coldewey.

18. Tom Warren, "Telegram Temporarily Removed from Apple's App Store Due to 'Inappropriate Content,'" The Verge, February 1, 2018, https://www.theverge.com/2018/2/1/16958990/telegram-apple-app-store-removal-inappropriate-content.

19. Tom Warren, "Inside the Bitter YouTube Battle between Microsoft and Google," The Verge, August 16, 2013,

https://www.theverge.com/2013/8/16/4627342/microsoft-google-battle-over-youtube-windows-phone.

THE INFLUENCERS

1. Claire Allbright, "A Russian Facebook Page Organized a Protest in Texas. A Different Russian Page Launched the Counterprotest.," November 1, 2017, https://www.texastribune.org/2017/11/01/russian-facebook-page-organized-protest-texas-different-russian-page-l/.

2. Allbright.

3. Gabe O'Connor and Avie Schneider, "How Russian Twitter Bots Pumped Out Fake News During The 2016 Election," NPR.org, accessed April 22, 2019, https://www.npr.org/sections/alltechconsidered/2017/04/03/52250 3844/how-russian-twitter-bots-pumped-out-fake-news-during-the-2016-election.

4. Kevin Warwick and Huma Shah, "How the 'Good Life' Is Threatened in Cyberspace," February 2012, https://www.academia.edu/2380537/How_the_Good_Life_is_Threat ened_in_Cyberspace.

5. Marty Swant, "Twitter Says Users Now Trust Influencers Nearly as Much as Their Friends," May 10, 2016, https://www.adweek.com/digital/twitter-says-users-now-trust-influencers-nearly-much-their-friends-171367/.

6. Chengcheng Shao et al., "The Spread of Low-Credibility Content by Social Bots," *Nature Communications* 9, no. 1 (November 20, 2018): 4787, https://doi.org/10.1038/s41467-018-06930-7.

7. Tim Mak, "Russian Influence Campaign Sought To Exploit Americans' Trust In Local News," NPR.org, July 12, 2018, https://www.npr.org/2018/07/12/628085238/russian-influence-campaign-sought-to-exploit-americans-trust-in-local-news.

8. Amy Mitchell et al., "Trust and Accuracy of American News Organizations | Pew Research Center," July 7, 2016, https://www.journalism.org/2016/07/07/trust-and-accuracy/.

9. J. M. Porup, "How Mexican Twitter Bots Shut Down Dissent," *Motherboard* (blog), August 24, 2015, https://motherboard.vice.com/en_us/article/z4maww/how-mexican-twitter-bots-shut-down-dissent.

10. Alessandro Bessi and Emilio Ferrara, "Social Bots Distort the 2016 U.S.

Presidential Election Online Discussion," *First Monday* 21, no. 11 (November 3, 2016), https://doi.org/10.5210/fm.v21i11.7090.

11. Gabe O'Connor and Avie Schneider, "How Russian Twitter Bots Pumped Out Fake News During The 2016 Election."

12. Scott Shane, "The Fake Americans Russia Created to Influence the Election," *The New York Times*, January 20, 2018, sec. U.S., https://www.nytimes.com/2017/09/07/us/politics/russia-facebook-twitter-election.html.

13. "Saudi Bots Use 'Hashtag Poisoning' to Spread Propaganda," The Peninsula Online, February 5, 2018, https://www.thepeninsulaqatar.com/article/05/02/2018/Saudi-bots-use-%E2%80%98hashtag-poisoning%E2%80%99-to-spread-propaganda.

14. Adam Rawnsley, "Russian Trolls Denied Syrian Gas Attack—Before It Happened," April 12, 2018, sec. world, https://www.thedailybeast.com/russian-trolls-denied-syrian-gas-attackbefore-it-happened.

15. Michael Stone, "'The Bot Rot': Are Follower Numbers Real?," Forbes, February 9, 2018, https://www.forbes.com/sites/michaelstone/2018/02/09/the-bot-rot-are-follower-numbers-real/.

16. Lorenzo Franceschi-Bicchierai, "Up to 24 Million Instagram Accounts Are Spambots, Study Says," *Motherboard* (blog), June 30, 2015, https://motherboard.vice.com/en_us/article/wnj9vy/24-million-instagram-accounts-spambots-study.

17. Kerry Flynn, "Twitter Influencers Suspect a Bot 'Purge,'" Mashable, January 30, 2018, https://mashable.com/2018/01/29/twitter-bots-purge-influencers-accounts/.

18. Ryan Bort, "Almost Half of Trump's Twitter Followers Appear to Be Fake," Newsweek, May 30, 2017, https://www.newsweek.com/donald-trump-twitter-followers-fake-617873.

19. Simon Shuster and Sandra Ifraimova, "A Former Russian Troll Explains How to Spread Fake News," Time, February 21, 2018, http://time.com/5168202/russia-troll-internet-research-agency/.

20. U.S. Department of Justice, "Grand Jury Indicts Thirteen Russian Individuals and Three Russian Companies for Scheme to Interfere in the United States Political System," February 16, 2018,

https://www.justice.gov/opa/pr/grand-jury-indicts-thirteen-russian-individuals-and-three-russian-companies-scheme-interfere.

21. Craig Timberg and Elizabeth Dwoskin, "Twitter Is Sweeping out Fake Accounts like Never before, Putting User Growth at Risk," Washington Post, July 6, 2018, https://www.washingtonpost.com/technology/2018/07/06/twitter-is-sweeping-out-fake-accounts-like-never-before-putting-user-growth-risk/.

22. Craig Timberg and Elizabeth Dwoskin.

23. Sean Gourley, "Get Ready for the Robot Propaganda Machine," *Wired UK*, February 5, 2015, https://www.wired.co.uk/article/robot-propaganda.

24. Joseph Cox, "I Bought a Russian Bot Army for Under $100," September 13, 2017, https://www.thedailybeast.com/i-bought-a-russian-bot-army-for-under-dollar100.

25. Abby Ohlheiser, "Analysis | The #WalkAway Meme Is What Happens When Everything Is Viral and Nothing Matters," Washington Post, July 2, 2018, https://www.washingtonpost.com/news/the-intersect/wp/2018/07/02/the-walkaway-meme-is-what-happens-when-everything-is-viral-and-nothing-matters/.

26. Abby Ohlheiser.

27. Abby Ohlheiser.

28. Abby Ohlheiser.

29. U.S. Department of Justice, "Grand Jury Indicts Thirteen Russian Individuals and Three Russian Companies for Scheme to Interfere in the United States Political System."

THE PROPAGANDISTS

1. John Naughton, "How China Censors the Net: By Making Sure There's Too Much Information | John Naughton," *The Guardian*, June 16, 2018, sec. Opinion, https://www.theguardian.com/commentisfree/2018/jun/16/how-china-censors-internet-information.

2. Philip Elmer-Dewitt, "First Nation in Cyberspace," *Time*, December 6, 1993.

3. Naughton, "How China Censors the Net."

4. Marisa Endicott, "Propaganda's New Goals: Create Confusion, Sow Doubt," US News & World Report, January 31, 2017, https://www.usnews.com/news/national-news/articles/2017-01-31/russian-propagandas-new-goals-create-confusion-sow-doubt.

5. Marisa Endicott.

6. Tim Mak, "Russian Influence Campaign Sought To Exploit Americans' Trust In Local News."

7. Tim Mak.

8. Laura Sydell, "How Russian Propaganda Spreads On Social Media," NPR.org, October 29, 2017, https://www.npr.org/sections/alltechconsidered/2017/10/29/560461835/how-russian-propaganda-spreads-on-social-media.

9. Nick Bilton, "How ISIS Became the World's Deadliest Tech Start-Up | Vanity Fair," accessed July 1, 2018, https://www.vanityfair.com/news/2016/06/how-isis-became-the-worlds-deadliest-tech-start-up.

10. Renee DiResta, "How ISIS and Russia Manufactured Crowds on Social Media," Wired, March 8, 2018, https://www.wired.com/story/isis-russia-manufacture-crowds/.

11. DiResta.

12. J. M. Berger, "How ISIS Games Twitter," The Atlantic, June 16, 2014, https://www.theatlantic.com/international/archive/2014/06/isis-iraq-twitter-social-media-strategy/372856/.

13. Berger.

14. Rand Waltzman, "The U.S. Is Losing the Social Media War," Time, October 12, 2015, http://time.com/4064698/social-media-propaganda/.

15. Cori E. Dauber, "The TRUTH Is out There: Responding to Insurgent Disinformation and Deception Operations," February 28, 2009, https://usacac.army.mil/CAC2/MilitaryReview/Archives/English/MilitaryReview_20090228_art005.pdf.

THE FINDERS

1. Heather Timmons, "Censorship Is Free Speech When Search Engines Do It, a US Court Just Ruled," Quartz, March 28, 2014, https://qz.com/193029/a-us-court-just-ruled-that-censorship-by-

search-engines-is-a-form-of-free-speech/.

2. Timmons.

3. Anh-Minh Do, "Baidu Handles 5 BILLION Search Queries Per Day," Tech in Asia, March 1, 2013, https://www.techinasia.com/baidu-handles-5-billion-per-day.

4. Danny Sullivan, "Google Now Handles at Least 2 Trillion Searches per Year," Search Engine Land, May 24, 2016, https://searchengineland.com/google-now-handles-2-999-trillion-searches-per-year-250247.

5. Timmons, "Censorship Is Free Speech When Search Engines Do It, a US Court Just Ruled."

6. Adam Raff, "Opinion | Search, but You May Not Find," *The New York Times*, December 27, 2009, sec. Opinion, https://www.nytimes.com/2009/12/28/opinion/28raff.html.

7. Andrew Harrer, "Amazon Scraps a Secret A.I. Recruiting Tool That Showed Bias against Women," CNBC, October 10, 2018, https://www.cnbc.com/2018/10/10/amazon-scraps-a-secret-ai-recruiting-tool-that-showed-bias-against-women.html.

8. Andrew Harrer.

9. Marguerite Reardon, "House Republicans Accuse Google of Liberal Bias," CNET, December 11, 2018, https://www.cnet.com/news/house-republicans-accuse-google-of-liberal-bias/.

10. Olivia Solon and Sam Levin, "How Google's Search Algorithm Spreads False Information with a Rightwing Bias," *The Guardian*, December 16, 2016, sec. Technology, https://www.theguardian.com/technology/2016/dec/16/google-autocomplete-rightwing-bias-algorithm-political-propaganda.

11. Solon and Levin.

12. Solon and Levin.

13. Kimberly Coleman, "This Is How Redditors Manipulated Google's Image Search Engine," *EDGY_ Labs* (blog), December 9, 2016, https://edgy.app/google-search-engine-influenced-reddit.

14. Solon and Levin, "How Google's Search Algorithm Spreads False Information with a Rightwing Bias."

15. Abby Ohlheiser, "How 'Googling It' Can Send Conservatives Down Secret Rabbit Holes of Alternative Facts," *Medium* (blog), May 29, 2018, https://medium.com/thewashingtonpost/how-googling-it-can-send-

conservatives-down-secret-rabbit-holes-of-alternative-facts-4bc7b7699c1e.

16. Rob Price, "Google Promoted a Fake Conspiracy Theory That Obama Was Planning a Coup," Business Insider, March 6, 2017, https://www.businessinsider.com/google-home-claims-obama-planning-communist-coup-conspiracy-theories-featured-snippets-2017-3.

17. Jon Porter, "DuckDuckGo Hits New Milestone of 30 Million Private Searches per Day," The Verge, October 12, 2018, https://www.theverge.com/2018/10/12/17967224/duckduckgo-daily-searches-privacy-30-million-2018.

18. Gabriel Weinberg, "Gabriel Weinberg's Answer to Why Should I Use DuckDuckGo Instead of Google? · Quora," Quora, October 8, 2018, https://www.quora.com/Why-should-I-use-DuckDuckGo-instead-of-Google/answer/Gabriel-Weinberg.

19. Reardon, "House Republicans Accuse Google of Liberal Bias."

20. Reardon.

THE TRACKERS

1. Charles Duhigg, "How Companies Learn Your Secrets," *The New York Times*, February 16, 2012, sec. Magazine, https://www.nytimes.com/2012/02/19/magazine/shopping-habits.html.

2. Duhigg.

3. Duhigg.

4. Duhigg.

5. Caitlyn Renee Miller, "I Bought a Report on Everything That's Known About Me Online," The Atlantic, June 6, 2017, https://www.theatlantic.com/technology/archive/2017/06/online-data-brokers/529281/.

6. ublock Origin Development Team, *UBlock Origin: An Efficient Blocker for Chromium and Firefox. Fast and Lean. · Gorhill/UBlock*, JavaScript, 2019, https://github.com/gorhill/uBlock.

7. Christopher A. Summers, Rob Smith, and Rebecca Walker Reczek, "An Audience of One: Behaviorally Targeted Ads as Implied Social Labels," *Journal of Consumer Research* 43 (February 24, 2016): 156–78,

https://doi.org/10.1093/jcr/ucw012.

8. A. Summers, Smith, and Walker Reczek.

9. A. Summers, Smith, and Walker Reczek.

10. Joseph Turow et al., "Americans Roundly Reject Tailored Political Advertising," *Annenberg School for Communication, University of Pennsylvania*, July 1, 2012, https://repository.upenn.edu/asc_papers/398.

11. Solon and Levin, "How Google's Search Algorithm Spreads False Information with a Rightwing Bias."

12. Alex Hern, "Facebook 'dark Ads' Can Swing Political Opinions, Research Shows," *The Guardian*, July 31, 2017, sec. Technology, https://www.theguardian.com/technology/2017/jul/31/facebook-dark-ads-can-swing-opinions-politics-research-shows.

13. Hern.

14. Bryan Gardiner, "You'll Be Outraged at How Easy It Was to Get You to Click on This Headline," *WIRED*, December 18, 2015, https://www.wired.com/2015/12/psychology-of-clickbait/

15. Molly Wood, Stephanie Hughes, and Shaheen Ainpour, "Why Federal Regulations Don't Apply to Online Political Campaign Ads," March 6, 2018, http://www.marketplace.org/2018/03/06/tech/bringing-campaign-ad-laws-broadband-speed.

16. Molly Wood, Stephanie Hughes, and Shaheen Ainpour.

17. Jennifer Valentino-DeVries, "Facebook's Ad Transparency Experiment Can Still Mislead Users on Advertiser's Identity, Review Finds," January 31, 2018, https://www.theglobeandmail.com/news/national/facebooks-experiment-in-ad-transparency-can-still-mislead-users-on-advertisers-identity-review-finds/article37801018/.

18. Jennifer Valentino-DeVries.

19. William Turton, "We Posed as 100 Senators to Run Ads on Facebook. Facebook Approved All of Them.," *Vice News* (blog), October 30, 2018, https://news.vice.com/en_us/article/xw9n3q/we-posed-as-100-senators-to-run-ads-on-facebook-facebook-approved-all-of-them.

THE FAKERS

1. Aaron Rupar, "White House Press Secretary Uses Fake Infowars Video to Justify Banning CNN Reporter," Vox, November 8, 2018, https://www.vox.com/2018/11/8/18074966/sarah-sanders-infowars-cnn-jim-acosta-banned.

2. Sophie Nightingale, Kimberley Wade, and Derrick G Watson, "Can People Identify Original and Manipulated Photos of Real-World Scenes?," *Cognitive Research: Principles and Implications* 2 (June 12, 2017), https://doi.org/10.1186/s41235-017-0067-2.

3. William Wan, "Many People Can't Tell When Photos Are Fake. Can You?," Washington Post, July 17, 2017, https://www.washingtonpost.com/news/speaking-of-science/wp/2017/07/17/many-people-cant-tell-when-photos-are-fake-can-you/.

4. J. Thies et al., "Face2Face: Real-Time Face Capture and Reenactment of RGB Videos," in *2016 IEEE Conference on Computer Vision and Pattern Recognition (CVPR)*, 2016, 2387–95, https://doi.org/10.1109/CVPR.2016.262.

5. Rob Price, "AI and CGI Will Transform Information Warfare, Boost Hoaxes, and Escalate Revenge Porn," Business Insider, August 12, 2017, https://www.businessinsider.com/cgi-ai-fake-video-audio-news-hoaxes-information-warfare-revenge-porn-2017-8.

6. Drew Harwell, "Fake-Porn Videos Are Being Weaponized to Harass and Humiliate Women: 'Everybody Is a Potential Target,'" Washington Post, December 30, 2018, https://www.washingtonpost.com/technology/2018/12/30/fake-porn-videos-are-being-weaponized-harass-humiliate-women-everybody-is-potential-target/.

7. Rebecca Ruiz, "Deepfakes Are about to Make Revenge Porn so Much Worse," Mashable, June 24, 2018, https://mashable.com/article/deepfakes-revenge-porn-domestic-violence/.

8. Adi Robertson, "Reddit Bans 'Deepfakes' AI Porn Communities," The Verge, February 7, 2018, https://www.theverge.com/2018/2/7/16982046/reddit-deepfakes-ai-celebrity-face-swap-porn-community-ban.

9. Ruiz, "Deepfakes Are about to Make Revenge Porn so Much Worse."

10. Tim Mak, "Can You Believe Your Own Ears? With New 'Fake News' Tech, Not Necessarily," NPR.org, April 4, 2018,

https://www.npr.org/2018/04/04/599126774/can-you-believe-your-own-ears-with-new-fake-news-tech-not-necessarily.

11. Tim Mak.

12. sp_a, "Sp.a on Twitter: 'Trump Heeft Een Boodschap Voor Alle Belgen... #Klimaatpetitie Https://T.Co/Kf7nIaDOKj' / Twitter," Twitter, May 20, 2018, https://twitter.com/sp_a/status/998089909369016325.

13. Hans von der Burchard, "Belgian Socialist Party Circulates 'Deep Fake' Donald Trump Video," POLITICO, May 21, 2018, https://www.politico.eu/article/spa-donald-trump-belgium-paris-climate-agreement-belgian-socialist-party-circulates-deep-fake-trump-video/.

14. Oscar Schwartz, "You Thought Fake News Was Bad? Deep Fakes Are Where Truth Goes to Die," *The Guardian*, November 12, 2018, sec. Technology, https://www.theguardian.com/technology/2018/nov/12/deep-fakes-fake-news-truth.

15. Burchard, "Belgian Socialist Party Circulates 'Deep Fake' Donald Trump Video."

16. Schwartz, "You Thought Fake News Was Bad?"

17. William Wan, "Many People Can't Tell When Photos Are Fake. Can You?"

18. usminority, "Brandon Straka on Twitter: 'These Memes Have Nothing 2do w/ the #WalkAway Campaign. They're Being Circulated by the Left as Evidence That #WalkAway Is Paid Actors.   So, in a Rare Moment of Agreement, I Am on the Same Page as Those on the Left- This Is Fake. These r Not from the #WalkAway Campaign. Https://T.Co/NN3kNlBAsr' / Twitter," Twitter, July 24, 2018, https://twitter.com/usminority/status/1021614263322992641.

19. Daniela Sternitzky-Di Napoli, "Fake Photo of Trump Saving Cats during Harvey Takes over the Internet," Houston Chronicle, September 16, 2017, https://www.chron.com/news/houston-texas/article/Fake-photo-Trump-saving-cats-during-Harvey-12203385.php.

20. Grace Hauck, "'Pizzagate' Shooter Sentenced to 4 Years in Prison," CNN, June 22, 2017, https://www.cnn.com/2017/06/22/politics/pizzagate-sentencing/index.html.

21. "What Is the QAnon Conspiracy Theory?," CBS News, accessed August 3, 2018, https://www.cbsnews.com/news/what-is-the-qanon-conspiracy-theory/.

22. Caitlin Dewey, "6 in 10 of You Will Share This Link without Reading It, a New, Depressing Study Says," Washington Post, June 16, 2016, https://www.washingtonpost.com/news/the-intersect/wp/2016/06 /16/six-in-10-of-you-will-share-this-link-without-reading-it-according-to-a-new-and-depressing-study/.

23. Maksym Gabielkov et al., "Social Clicks: What and Who Gets Read on Twitter?," in *Proceedings of the 2016 ACM SIGMETRICS International Conference on Measurement and Modeling of Computer Science*, SIGMETRICS '16 (New York, NY, USA: ACM, 2016), 179–192, https:// doi.org/10.1145/2896377.2901462.

24. Caitlin Dewey, "6 in 10 of You Will Share This Link without Reading It, a New, Depressing Study Says."

25. Jesse Singal, "People Spread Fake News Because They Believe Anything Their Friends Post," Intelligencer, March 21, 2017, http://nymag.com/ intelligencer/2017/03/fake-news-spreads-because-people-trust-their-friends-too-much.html.

26. Jeff Stibel, "Fake News: How Our Brains Lead Us into Echo Chambers That Promote Racism and Sexism," USA TODAY, May 15, 2018, https://www.usatoday.com/story/money/columnist/2018/05/15/fa ke-news-social-media-confirmation-bias-echo-chambers/533857002/.

27. Newton, "The Secret Lives of Facebook Moderators in America."

THE BAITED

1. Chris Smith, "Jon Stewart on 16 Years of The Daily Show and His Directorial Debut Rosewater," Intelligencer, November 3, 2014, http:// nymag.com/daily/intelligencer/2014/10/jon-stewart-rosewater-in-conversation.html.

2. Bryan Gardiner, "You'll Be Outraged at How Easy It Was to Get You to Click on This Headline," *WIRED*, December 18, 2015, https://www.wired.com/2015/12/psychology-of-clickbait/

3. "Clickbait | Definition of Clickbait in English by Oxford Dictionaries," in *Oxford Dictionaries*, accessed November 20, 2018, https://en.oxforddictionaries.com/definition/clickbait.

4. Gabielkov et al., "Social Clicks."

5. Drake Baer, "The Science Behind Why Facebook Is So Addictive," Business Insider, November 13, 2014, https://www.businessinsider.com/science-behind-why-facebook-is-

addictive-2014-11.

6. "How Americans Get Their News," American Press Institute, March 17, 2014, https://www.americanpressinstitute.org/publications/reports/survey-research/how-americans-get-news/.

7. Ben Smith, "Why BuzzFeed Doesn't Do Clickbait," *Buzzfeed*, November 6, 2014, https://www.buzzfeed.com/bensmith/why-buzzfeed-doesnt-do-clickbait

8. Angèle Christin, "When It Comes to Chasing Clicks, Journalists Say One Thing but Feel Pressure to Do Another," *Nieman Lab* (blog), August 28, 2014, https://www.niemanlab.org/2014/08/when-it-comes-to-chasing-clicks-journalists-say-one-thing-but-feel-pressure-to-do-another/.

9. Bill Murphy, Jr., "Researchers Studied 1.67 Million Clickbait Headlines. What They Learned Will Completely Shock You," Inc.com, March 22, 2018, https://www.inc.com/bill-murphy-jr/these-researchers-studied-167-million-clickbait-headlines-what-they-found-will-totally-shock-you.html.

10. Eli Saslow, "'Nothing on This Page Is Real': How Lies Become Truth in Online America," Washington Post, November 17, 2018, https://www.washingtonpost.com/national/nothing-on-this-page-is-real-how-lies-become-truth-in-online-america/2018/11/17/edd44cc8-e85a-11e8-bbdb-72fdbf9d4fed_story.html.

11. Saslow.

12. Saslow.

13. Terrence McCoy, "For the 'New Yellow Journalists,' Opportunity Comes in Clicks and Bucks," Washington Post, November 20, 2016, https://www.washingtonpost.com/national/for-the-new-yellow-journalists-opportunity-comes-in-clicks-and-bucks/2016/11/20/d58d036c-adbf-11e6-8b45-f8e493f06fcd_story.html.

14. Terrence McCoy.

15. Terrence McCoy.

16. Terrence McCoy.

17. Craig Silverman, "This Analysis Shows How Viral Fake Election News Stories Outperformed Real News On Facebook," BuzzFeed News, November 16, 2016, https://www.buzzfeednews.com/article/craigsilverman/viral-fake-election-news-outperformed-real-news-on-facebook.

18. Kaya Yurieff, "Facebook Steps up Fake News Fight with 'Related Articles,'" CNNMoney, August 3, 2017, https://money.cnn.com/2017/08/03/technology/facebook-related-articles/index.html.

THE ADDICTS

1. Natasha Singer, "Can't Put Down Your Device? That's by Design," *The New York Times*, December 21, 2017, sec. Technology, https://www.nytimes.com/2015/12/06/technology/personaltech/cant-put-down-your-device-thats-by-design.html.

2. Elizabeth Cohen, "Five Clues That You Are Addicted to Facebook · CNN.Com," CNN, April 23, 2009, http://www.cnn.com/2009/HEALTH/04/23/ep.facebook.addict/index.html.

3. Noah Kulwin, "An Apology for the Internet — From the Architects Who Built It," Intelligencer, April 13, 2018, http://nymag.com/intelligencer/2018/04/an-apology-for-the-internet-from-the-people-who-built-it.html.

4. "GrowthHackers," GrowthHackers, accessed August 10, 2018, https://growthhackers.com/.

5. Simon Parkin, "Has Dopamine Got Us Hooked on Tech?," *The Observer*, March 4, 2018, sec. Technology, https://www.theguardian.com/technology/2018/mar/04/has-dopamine-got-us-hooked-on-tech-facebook-apps-addiction.

6. Parkin.

7. Paul Lewis, "'Our Minds Can Be Hijacked': The Tech Insiders Who Fear a Smartphone Dystopia," *The Guardian*, October 6, 2017, sec. Technology, https://www.theguardian.com/technology/2017/oct/05/smartphone-addiction-silicon-valley-dystopia.

8. Lewis.

9. Eric P. S. Baumer et al., "Missing Photos, Suffering Withdrawal, or Finding Freedom? How Experiences of Social Media Non-Use Influence the Likelihood of Reversion," *Social Media + Society* 1, no. 2 (July 1, 2015): 2056305115614851, https://doi.org/10.1177/2056305115614851.

10. Lewis, "'Our Minds Can Be Hijacked.'"

11. Olivia Solon, "Ex-Facebook president Sean Parker: site made to exploit human 'vulnerability,'" *The Guardian*, November 9, 2017,

https://www.theguardian.com/technology/2017/nov/09/facebook-sean-parker-vulnerability-brain-psychology

12. Bill Snyder, "Chamath Palihapitiya: Why Failing Fast Fails," Stanford Graduate School of Business, December 12, 2017, https://www.gsb.stanford.edu/insights/chamath-palihapitiya-why-failing-fast-fails.

13. Lewis, "'Our Minds Can Be Hijacked.'"

14. Lewis.

15. Lewis.

16. Lewis.

17. Singer, "Can't Put Down Your Device?"

THE INHABITANTS

1. Clifford Stoll, "Why the Web Won't Be Nirvana," *Newsweek*, February 26, 1995, https://www.newsweek.com/clifford-stoll-why-web-wont-be-nirvana-185306.

2. Omar Sinan, "How to build a simple Twitter bot in 17 lines of code," DEV Community, accessed July 21, 2019, https://dev.to/omarhashimoto/how-to-build-a-simple-twitter-bot-in-17-lines-ofcode-2aan.

3. Jacqueline Detwiler, "Are Influencers Worth Your Money? We Went Undercover to Find Out," *Entrepreneur - US Edition*, February 21, 2018, https://www.entrepreneur.com/article/308694.

4. Drew Harwell, "Fake-Porn Videos Are Being Weaponized to Harass and Humiliate Women: 'Everybody Is a Potential Target,'" *Washington Post*, December 30, 2018, https://www.washingtonpost.com/technology/2018/12/30/fake-porn-videos-are-being-weaponized-harass-humiliate-women-everybody-is-potential-target/.

5. Jay Hoffmann, "The First Thing That Ever Sold Online Was Pizza," The History of the Web, July 30, 2018, https://thehistoryoftheweb.com/postscript/pizzanet/.

6. Monica Riese, "The definitive history of social media," *The Daily Dot*, February 24, 2017, https://www.dailydot.com/debug/history-of-social-media/.

7. David Cole, "The ACLU's Longstanding Commitment to Defending

Speech We Hate," American Civil Liberties Union, June 23, 2018, https://www.aclu.org/blog/free-speech/aclus-longstanding-commitment-defending-speech-we-hate.

8. Clifford Stoll, "Why the Web Won't Be Nirvana."

9. Megan Graham, "Digital ad revenue in the US surpassed $100 billion for the first time in 2018," *CNBC*, May 7, 2019, https://www.cnbc.com/2019/05/07/digital-ad-revenue-in-the-us-topped-100-billion-for-the-first-time.html

10. Benedict Carey, "How Fiction Becomes Fact on Social Media," *The New York Times*, October 20, 2017, https://www.nytimes.com/2017/10/20/health/social-media-fake-news.html

11. Andrew Anthony, "Yuval Noah Harari: 'The Idea of Free Information Is Extremely Dangerous,'" *The Observer*, August 5, 2018, sec. Culture, https://www.theguardian.com/culture/2018/aug/05/yuval-noah-harari-free-information-extremely-dangerous-interview-21-lessons.

12. Aaron Smith and Monica Anderson, "Social Media Use 2018: Demographics and Statistics | Pew Research Center," March 1, 2018, https://www.pewinternet.org/2018/03/01/social-media-use-in-2018/.

13. Darrell Etherington, "Amazon AWS S3 Outage Is Breaking Things for a Lot of Websites and Apps," *TechCrunch* (blog), February 28, 2017, http://social.techcrunch.com/2017/02/28/amazon-aws-s3-outage-is-breaking-things-for-a-lot-of-websites-and-apps/.

14. Matthew Prince, "Why We Terminated Daily Stormer," *The Cloudflare Blog* (blog), August 16, 2017, https://blog.cloudflare.com/why-we-terminated-daily-stormer/.

15. Casey Newton, "The Secret Lives of Facebook Moderators in America," The Verge, February 25, 2019, https://www.theverge.com/2019/2/25/18229714/cognizant-facebook-content-moderator-interviews-trauma-working-conditions-arizona.

16. Barbara Ortutay, "Facebook Kills 'trending' Topics, Tests Breaking News Label," AP NEWS, June 1, 2018, https://apnews.com/91af6216e641494eabda1b17463147d3.

17. Renee DiResta, "Free Speech Is Not the Same As Free Reach," *Wired*, August 30, 2018, https://www.wired.com/story/free-speech-is-not-the-same-as-free-reach/.

18. Paul Lewis, "'Our Minds Can Be Hijacked': The Tech Insiders Who Fear a

Smartphone Dystopia," *The Guardian*, October 6, 2017, sec. Technology, https://www.theguardian.com/technology/2017/oct/05/smartphone-addiction-silicon-valley-dystopia.

19. Christopher A. Bail et al., "Exposure to Opposing Views Can Increase Political Polarization: Evidence from a Large-Scale Field Experiment on Social Media," preprint (SocArXiv, March 21, 2018), https://doi.org/10.31235/osf.io/4ygux.

20. Caitlin Dewey, "6 in 10 of You Will Share This Link without Reading It, a New, Depressing Study Says," Washington Post, June 16, 2016, https://www.washingtonpost.com/news/the-intersect/wp/2016/06/16/six-in-10-of-you-will-share-this-link-without-reading-it-according-to-a-new-and-depressing-study/.

21. Zeynep Tufekci, "It's the (Democracy-Poisoning) Golden Age of Free Speech," *Wired*, January 16, 2018, https://www.wired.com/story/free-speech-issue-tech-turmoil-new-censorship/.

22. Avi Asher-Schapiro, "YouTube and Facebook Are Removing Evidence of Atrocities, Jeopardizing Cases Against War Criminals," *The Intercept* (blog), November 2, 2017, https://theintercept.com/2017/11/02/war-crimes-youtube-facebook-syria-rohingya/.

23. Rob Price, "Google Promoted a Fake Conspiracy Theory That Obama Was Planning a Coup," Business Insider, March 6, 2017, https://www.businessinsider.com/google-home-claims-obama-planning-communist-coup-conspiracy-theories-featured-snippets-2017-3.

24. Russell Brandom, "Facebook's Report Abuse Button Has Become a Tool of Global Oppression," September 2, 2014, https://www.theverge.com/2014/9/2/6083647/facebook-s-report-abuse-button-has-become-a-tool-of-global-oppression.

25. Adam Rawnsley, "Russian Trolls Denied Syrian Gas Attack—Before It Happened," April 12, 2018, sec. world, https://www.thedailybeast.com/russian-trolls-denied-syrian-gas-attackbefore-it-happened.

26. Simon Shuster and Sandra Ifraimova, "A Former Russian Troll Explains How to Spread Fake News," Time, February 21, 2018, http://time.com/5168202/russia-troll-internet-research-agency/.

27. Tim Mak, "Russian Influence Campaign Sought To Exploit Americans' Trust In Local News," NPR.org, July 12, 2018,

https://www.npr.org/2018/07/12/628085238/russian-influence-campaign-sought-to-exploit-americans-trust-in-local-news.

28. Claire Allbright, "A Russian Facebook Page Organized a Protest in Texas. A Different Russian Page Launched the Counterprotest.," November 1, 2017, https://www.texastribune.org/2017/11/01/russian-facebook-page-organized-protest-texas-different-russian-page-1/.

29. Napoli, "Fake Photo of Trump Saving Cats during Harvey Takes over the Internet."

30. Rebecca Ruiz, "Deepfakes Are about to Make Revenge Porn so Much Worse," Mashable, June 24, 2018, https://mashable.com/article/deepfakes-revenge-porn-domestic-violence/.

31. Tim Mak, "Can You Believe Your Own Ears? With New 'Fake News' Tech, Not Necessarily," NPR.org, April 4, 2018, https://www.npr.org/2018/04/04/599126774/can-you-believe-your-own-ears-with-new-fake-news-tech-not-necessarily.

32. Hans von der Burchard, "Belgian Socialist Party Circulates 'Deep Fake' Donald Trump Video," POLITICO, May 21, 2018, https://www.politico.eu/article/spa-donald-trump-belgium-paris-climate-agreement-belgian-socialist-party-circulates-deep-fake-trump-video/.

www.ingramcontent.com/pod-product-compliance
Lightning Source LLC
Chambersburg PA
CBHW031220050326
40689CB00009B/1402